T0163282

Plurality and Progress

Peter Wagner

Plurality and Progress

Modernity in political philosophy and historical sociology

NSU Summertalk vol. 6 | 2010

An NSU Series Edited by:
Claus Krogholm

NSU Press

To Asteris Stefan

Published in Sweden by NSU Press
Norra Vallgatan 16
SE-211 25 Malmö, SWEDEN
http://www.nsuweb.net

Produced by Söderströms Förlag
Georgsgatan 29A, 2 vån
PO Box 870
FI-00101 Helsingfors, FINLAND
http://www.soderstrom.fi

Printed by Nord Print Ab
Helsingfors, 2010

Distributed by Århus University Press
Langelandsgade 177
8200 Århus N DENMARK
http://www.unipress.dk

ISBN 978-87-87564-20-5

Contents

Preface   7

1

Analysing Modernity, Understanding the Present   11

2

From Convergence and Stability to Plurality and Transformations   21

3

Successive Modernities and the Idea of Progress   39

4

Trajectories of Modernity: Comparing European and
non-European Varieties   59

5

Towards a World Sociology of Modernity   85

References   96

PREFACE

This book would not have existed without the occasion that solicited it. Thus, it should begin with a word of thanks to the organizers of the Nordic Summer University in Tyrifjord in July 2009, and in particular to Ingerid Straume, for providing the occasion to reflect anew about the ways in which social and political thought and research can help understanding our present condition.

Only now that the Tyrifjord lectures have acquired the shape they find in this book can I fully appreciate the consequences of having been asked to give them at this particular moment. In the summer of 2009 I thought to have developed an approach to 'modernity as experience and interpretation' (Wagner 2008) as a rather novel way of linking comparative-historical sociology to social and political philosophy. This moment of conclusion should mark an interim in which new questions arose – or rather: in which old questions returned to the agenda. The most important ones are these: if there is a plurality of modern forms of socio-political organisation, what does this entail for our time-honoured idea of progress, or in other words: for our hope that the future world can be better than the present one? And: if despite all awareness of the risk of Eurocentrism our concept of modernity is to some extent inextricably linked to the history of Europe (or: the West), how can we analyse and compare European and non-European modernities in a 'symmetric', non-biased way? These are questions of which I had necessarily been always aware but which I had not yet explicitly addressed before the Tyrifjord lectures. The provisional answers I now give to them can be found in chapters three and four below.

These answers need a background and a context. Chapter two elaborates systematically on the recent change in perceptions of modernity: from convergence and stability to plurality and transformations. It thus provides the background against which the questions about progress and the comparison of co-existing varieties of modernity can be addressed. The context of writing is one of a particular urgency. The thinking about modernity has always aimed at the global and the universal. Modernity was seen as normatively and functionally superior to other forms of socio-political organization. Universal claims were made in its name, and its worldwide diffusion was expected. It is now, however, in our era of so-called globalisation, of radical time-space compression, that these claims and expectations become inescapable in so many walks of life and for many more people than ever. Chapter one discusses the global nature of modernity by way of an introduction. The last chapter, chapter five, returns to this issue in terms of a brief programmatic exploration of the spatio-temporal aspects that a future world sociology of modernity would need to address.

Some of the following reflections have been developed further between the summer of 2009 and the moment when this book goes to print. Thanks are due to Mikael Carleheden for asking for a contribution to an issue of *Distinktion. Scandinavian Journal for Social Theory* on 'successive modernities', which has been used for chapter three. Chapter two was written while lecturing at the Université catholique de Louvain-la-neuve in March 2010, and I would like to thank Jean de Munck for having created this occasion. Parts of chapter four will appear in the *European Journal of Social Theory* in an issue devoted to the work of Johann Arnason who has been a discussant for matters of modernity over more ten years now. Chapter five contains an outline of a contribution for a volume honouring the work of Björn Wittrock to whom the same applies for more than a quarter-century. Parts of chapter one will also appear in the *Encyclopedia of Globalization*, edited by George Ritzer (Oxford: Wiley-Blackwell, in preparation 2012) and parts of chapter two in the *Handbook of Contemporary Social and Political Theory*, edited by Gerard Delanty and Stephen Turner (London: Routledge, forthcoming 2011).

Trento, May 2010

1

Analysing Modernity, Understanding the Present

The most common – even though far from unproblematic – view about modernity holds that this term refers to a novel kind of society that emerged from a sequence of major transformations in Europe and North America culminating in the industrial and democratic revolutions in the late eighteenth and early nineteenth centuries. Significantly, this view often entails both that these transformations catapulted Europe (or the West) to the front position in the course of world history and that the thus established Western model would diffuse worldwide because of its inherent superiority. Thinking about modernity thus meant thinking about globalisation, even though these terms have come into frequent use only since the 1980s and 1990s respectively.

Global – or universal – significance was claimed for European modernity from the very beginning. A key event in the formation of what we consider as modern Europe was the so-called discovery of the Americas with their hitherto unknown populations, and this event triggered European reflections about the nature of humankind and provided a background to philosophical speculations about the 'state of nature', as in John Locke's *Second treatise on government* (1690). From René Descartes's *Discourse on method* (1637) onwards, Enlightenment thought claimed to have established the very few, but absolutely firm foundations on which universal knowledge could be erected, most basically freedom and reason. The American and French revolutions were seen as having inescapably introduced humanity to liberal democracy, based on individual rights and popular sovereignty. Already in his *Democracy in America* of the 1830s, Alexis de Tocqueville considered equal universal suffrage as the *telos* of political history. And from Adam Smith's *Wealth of nations* (1776) to the mid-nineteenth century, political economists claimed to have discovered in market self-regulation an absolutely superior form of economic organization. In the *Communist Manifesto* (1848), Karl Marx and Friedrich Engels provided an image of economic globalisation whose evocative power has not been surpassed ever since.

A common basic understanding of modernity underlies this debate that stretches over two centuries and addresses very different aspects of human social life. Modernity is the belief in the freedom of the human being – natural and inalienable, as many philosophers presumed – and in the human capacity to reason combined with the intelligibility of the world, that is, its amenability to human reason. In a first step towards concreteness, this basic commitment translates into the principles of individual and collective self-determination and in the expectation of ever increasing mastery of nature and ever more reasonable interaction between human beings. The *Declaration of the rights of man and of the citizen* (1793) as well as the granting of commercial freedom can be understood as applications of these underlying principles of modernity as can the technical transformations captured by the term Industrial Revolution.

These principles were seen as *universal*, on the one hand, because they contained normative claims to which, one presumed, every human being would subscribe, and on the other, because they were deemed to permit the creation of functionally superior arrangements for major aspects of human social life, most importantly maybe the satisfaction of human needs in market-driven production and the rational government of collective matters through law-based and hierarchically organised administration. Furthermore, they were seen as *globalizing* in their application because of the interpretative and practical power of normativity and functionality.

None of these claims, however, was straightforwardly accepted. Even though the intellectual commitment to these principles was possibly widespread, considerable doubts existed about the possibility or probability of translating these principles into institutional arrangements without considerable modifications and losses. Among the early critical reflections, only two shall be mentioned. Immanuel Kant was committed to the idea of enlightened and accountable government and expected the republican principle (though not the democratic one) to flourish worldwide. However, he did not believe in what might have been considered the crowning of such process, the creation of a world republic, but argued for the normative superiority of a global federation of republics instead (*On perpetual peace*, 1795). Karl Marx's 'critique of political economy' (thus the subtitle of *Capital*, 1867), in turn, undermined the belief that the transformation of the human being into a market agent was based on the principles of liberty and equality, as political economy had suggested. This novel social formation, which he referred to as bourgeois society, rather divided humankind into two classes, the owners of means of production and those who had only their labour power to sell, who stood in an increasingly antagonistic relation to each other.

By the beginning of the twentieth century, the trajectory of European (or Western) societies had separated so considerably from those of other parts of the world that the particularity of 'Occidental rationalism', as Max Weber put it – not without hesitation – in the introduction to his comparative sociology of world-religions (1920, now mostly read as the preface to *The Protestant ethic*), had become a key topic of historico-sociological investigation (for a recent analysis see Pomeranz 2000). The ambiguity of Weber's terminological choice should stay with the debate on modernity ever since. Weber seemed to claim both that rationalization had Western origins and even preconditions in Western cosmology *and* that it had 'universal significance', the latter not without adding the much overlooked parenthesis 'as we [presumably: the Westerners] are inclined to think'. Thus, it permitted both the promoters of modernization theory and those more recent authors and advocates of the theorem of multiple modernities to refer to Weber as the main source of inspiration. The former, headed by Talcott Parsons, suggested that the Western 'breakthrough' to modernity would (need to) be emulated by elites in other societies because of its normative and functional superiority and that therefore Western modernity would diffuse globally in processes of 'modernization and development', as the sociological jargon of the 1960s had it. The latter, inspired by Shmuel N. Eisenstadt, were not denying the 'universal significance' of Western social transformations since the 1700s, but held that the encounter of other civilizations with Western modernity did not lead to the mere diffusion of the Western model but rather to the proliferation of varieties of modernity generated by the encounter of different 'cultural programmes', which had consolidated much earlier, with Western ideas and practices.

The opposition between neo-modernization theory and the multiple modernities theorem, which marks current sociological debate on modernity, tends to sideline the third aspect of Weber's view of 'Occidental rationalism', namely a profound scepticism as to the fate of modernity. From this angle, Weber's reflections stand mid-stream in the tradition of a profound critique of modernity that was elaborated between the middle of the nineteenth and the middle of the twentieth century, with Karl Marx marking the beginning and Theodor W. Adorno the end, at least in its strong form, of this approach. Marx accepted the modern commitment to freedom and reason, as his expectation of a future 'free association of free human beings' demonstrates, but emphasized the impossibility to realize it under conditions of class domination. Market liberty in bourgeois society would lead to alienation and commodification, human beings relating to each other as things. Similarly, Weber saw the Protestant Reformation as an increase of individual autonomy, eliminating the institutional mediation of the church between the believer and God (*The Protestant ethic and the 'spirit' of capitalism*, 1904/05 and 1920). Once the social ethic associated with Protestantism, which emphasizes professional commitment and success, had contributed to bringing about the institutions of modern capitalism, however, a rationalized conduct of life would be imposed on the inhabitants of the 'dwellings made of steel' (the rendering of Weber's *stählernes Gehäuse* as 'iron cage' is rather misleading) characteristic of modernity. Adorno and Max Horkheimer (*Dialectics of Enlightenment*, 1944) provided the most extreme version of the theorem that the modern commitment to freedom and reason tends towards self-cancellation in its transformation into historically concrete social forms. They see the origins of this regression in the very philosophy of the Enlightenment that, in its insistence on the knowability of the world, transforms all qualities into mere quantities of the same and reduces the unknown to the status of a variable that is subject to the rules of mathematical equations. Such conceptualisation entered into a totalising alliance with industrial capitalism and produced, by the middle of the twentieth century, a society dominated by culture industry in which nothing could be heard or touched that had not been heard or touched before. Novelty and creativity were equally eliminated in societies as otherwise different as the mass culture of the United States (the text was written in Los Angeles), Nazi Germany or the Stalinist Soviet Union.

Such radical critiques of modernity gradually lost their persuasive power during the second post-war period of the twentieth century. An echo of them is found in Herbert Marcuse's analysis of 'one-dimensional man' and 'one-dimensional society' (1964), a diagnosis the reception of which in the student revolt of the late 1960s both demonstrated its appeal and tended to undermine is validity since the cultural revolution of '1968' arguably (re-) introduced a plurality of dimensions into the contemporary world. When Zygmunt Bauman revived the analysis of modernity as the obsessive attempt to create order and eliminate ambivalence (*Modernity and the holocaust*, 1989; *Modernity and ambivalence*, 1991), he did so partly in historical perspective offering a novel view on the Nazi genocide of the European Jews as an utterly modern phenomenon and partly situated his own writings at the exit of such organized modernity towards a post-modernity that reintroduced a concern with freedom, even though possibly a transformed and reduced one compared to earlier promises.

Such view about modernity undergoing a major transformation had indeed arisen from the late 1970s onwards, pioneered by Jean-François

Lyotard's *Postmodern condition* (1979). Lyotard radicalised the earlier sociological debate about a transformation from industrial to post-industrial society, promoted by authors such as Raymond Aron and Daniel Bell, by suggesting that the emerging social configuration was of such novelty that established concepts could no longer grasp it. Thus, his work contributed to launching a broad investigation, which has characterised much of political philosophy and comparative-historical sociology since, into the openness of the modern commitment to freedom and reason to a plurality of possibly interpretations. As a consequence, the earlier opposition between an affirmative view of modernity as the institutionalisation of freedom and reason, on the one hand, and the critical analysis of the self-cancellation of the modern normative commitment could now be re-read as evidence of, first, the ambiguity of the conceptual underpinnings of modernity and, second, the variety of possible translations of those commitments into institutionalised social practices, such as democracy and capitalism (Wagner 2008).

This insight gave new impetus to research on modernity. In political philosophy and social theory, the nature of the ambiguity and thus plurality of the modern commitment requires further investigation, not least with a view understanding the degree of openness of this commitment to interpretation and reviewing, not necessarily discarding, the universalist claims that had accompanied this commitment from its beginnings. In social research, the hypothesis of a recent major transformation of 'modern societies' between the 1960s and the present has informed many analyses from the mid-1980s onwards (for a major example see Boltanski and Chiapello 1999). Such research will need to address in particular the question whether such transformation, if it is ongoing, shows a specific direction breaking with or confirming the tendencies of modernity as they had been postulated in earlier theorizing. In the following, *chapter two* will address the question of the recent transformation of modernity and the plurality of modern forms from both the angles of political philosophy and of social research. *Chapter three* will take up the question of the historical direction of the transformations of modernity and will review the concept of progress in this light. Finally, comparative sociology of modernities will need to investigate whether the observable plurality of modern forms of socio-political organization is created from within specific historical trajectories and to explore the conditions for persistence of such plurality under current conditions of globalization – this is the task of *chapter four* (Wagner 2010).

This threefold task is remindful of the interpretations given to Weber's reflections on modernity, but the current condition of global modernity tends to sharpen the issues raised in earlier theorizing. The plurality of modern forms may lend itself to varieties of world-making projects (Karagiannis and Wagner 2007), but at the same time the often-observed homogenizing tendencies of globalisation may impose a return to the view of modernity as a single and unique form of social and political organisation that is without lasting alternatives. In that latter case, though, the critique of modernity may emerge in a new guise, as the critique of anomic individualization and reification that entails the risk of loss of world as a meaningful dwelling space, of worldlessness (see Arendt 1958 for the latter term; Honneth 2005 for the former). *Chapter five* will try to outline the contours of a world sociology of modernity that takes up the Weberian agenda in the light of the 'cultural problems' of today.

17

2

From Convergence and Stability to Plurality and Transformations

A concept with a history

Has modernity always been or has it recently become a key concern in social and political theory? In the former view, social and political theory emerged in Europe in the aftermath of the great transformations at the end of the eighteenth and the beginning of the nineteenth centuries. The novel social configuration that was forming as the combined effect of the Industrial Revolution and the French Revolution demanded novel means of analysis and interpretation; and social theory, in particular (without that term yet being coined), was the new intellectual tool to grasp its own present time, that is, its modernity. Proponents of the latter view, in turn, point to the fact that the noun 'modernity' has come into widespread use in social and political theory only in the last three decades. A look at this recent development provides us with an angle from which to grasp the longer history and the transformations of the concern with modernity in social and political theory.

Just over thirty years ago, in 1979, the French philosopher Jean-François Lyotard published a brief 'report on knowledge', which he had written at the request of the government of Québec, under the title *The postmodern condition*. Using data about the rapid diffusion of electronic information and communication technology and building on earlier arguments about the rise of 'post-industrial society', he argued that modern societies were undergoing a new major social transformation and that contemporary social theory was unable to grasp the nature of that monumental change. He criticized both mainstream social theorizing, epitomized by Parsonsian structural functionalism, and its critical alternative, as the exemplar for which he referred to Jürgen Habermas' work, for operating with reductionist and overly homogenizing concepts of the social bond and maintained that contemporary society was instead characterized by a multiplicity of social bonds best captured by the Wittgensteinian idea of a plurality of language games.

The little book contained provocative material for both political philosophy and empirical social research that, though much of it was not entirely new, had never appeared in such a condensed form. It suggested that modernity was neither functionally nor normatively superior to, or more advanced than, earlier social configurations, as almost all Western social and political theory had maintained for one and a half centuries. Furthermore, it denied the commonly held view that modernity undergoes predominantly linear evolution and reaches a stable state at full development. Rather, it was about to undergo a radical social transformation that invalidated many of its promises of human emancipation. And the outcome of this transformation was the co-existence of multiple forms of social bond in the shadow of a diffuse concern with performativity.

In reaction to this provocation, two strands of debate began to form in social and political theory during the 1980s. On the one hand, the foundations of modern reasoning and modern practices were re-assessed in more philosophically oriented debates, with Jürgen Habermas defending a sophisticated understanding of modernity in *The philosophical discourse of modernity* (1985) against critics such as Lyotard, Michel Foucault and Jacques Derrida, and Richard Rorty moving the pragmatist tradition close to the postmodern agenda in *Contingency, irony, solidarity* (1989). More sociologically oriented contributions focused on the question of the existence and nature of that new major social transformation that the theorem of postmodernity entailed. With *Risk society* (1986), Ulrich Beck was among the first to distinguish a first and simple modernity, in his view rather well captured by sociological debate up to the 1970s, from 'another', 'reflexive' modernity that was about to emerge. In a whole array of writings published between 1987 and 1992, as mentioned earlier, Zygmunt Bauman forcefully distinguished between a modernity obsessed with the creation of order and the elimination of ambivalence from an emerging post-modernity more gently interpreting rather than legislating human relations (*Legislators and interpreters*, 1987; *Modernity and the holocaust*, 1989; *Modernity and ambivalence*, 1991). From a focus on the critique of historical modernity, his more recent writings have turned towards critical assessments of the 'liquidity' of current social life (e.g., *Liquid modernity*, 2000). Avoiding any strong notions of an epochal break, Alain Touraine (*Critique de la modernité*, 1992) suggested that modernity had always been characterized by the two tendencies towards subjectivation and rationalization, but concern with the former now re-emerged after a long period of predominance of the latter.

These were the debates in which the noun 'modernity' was introduced in social theory and political philosophy, which hitherto had been content with using terms such as 'modern society', 'industrial society', or 'capitalist society' for their main object. The purpose of investigation did not change with the terminology; the analysis of contemporary social configurations and the relations between the human beings that form them remained the major task. However, the change of terminology signaled that there was a need to reassure oneself about the nature of this object and about the purpose of one's investigations.

The doubts about the stability and superiority of Western, 'modern society' were not confined to theoretical reflections during this period. The late 1970s and early 1980s were the years in which: the Iranian revolution brought an end to the idea that non-Western societies were just a bit behind on the same modernizing trajectory on which Western ones had embarked; the rise of the Japanese economy suggested that a capitalism with a non-Protestant cultural background could compete successfully with the allegedly more advanced economies; the rise of neo-liberal ideologies (monetarism and supply-side economics as they were then known) to governing power in the UK and the US and the concomitant failure of Keynesian economic policy by a socialist-led government in

France signaled the end of the optimism that market economies could smoothly be steered by national governments. Furthermore, these years were bracketed by the student, workers' and civil rights movements of the late 1960s that suddenly interrupted the tranquility of the apparent postwar social consensus, on the one side, and by the collapse of Soviet-style socialism between 1989 and 1991, on the other side. There was plenty of everyday evidence at hand that suggested the need to interrogate anew the contemporary human condition.

Against this double background, the adoption of the term 'modernity' expressed the need for a new language for interpreting the contemporary socio-political condition, or at least the need for posing the question whether a new language was required. The new debate clearly drew on and referred to the long tradition of analysis of 'modern society', but aimed at re-assessing that tradition in the light of new experiences that were increasingly being analyzed as a profound transformation of modernity. In the remainder of this chapter, I will first briefly discuss that which is now the 'pre-history' of the modernity debate, that is, the social and political theory of modern and capitalist society in both its affirmative and its critical strands since the great social transformations of the late eighteenth and early nineteenth centuries. This historical look will facilitate the analysis of the outcome of the recent re-assessment of modernity, which will be the second step, presented as the shift from an exclusively institutional to an interpretative analysis of modernity, which more than the former allows for plurality and transformability. Thirdly, this shift has given rise to a new opposition in most recent debate, which sees defenders of (neo-) modernization theory with persistent institutional emphasis reacting to the challenge from interpretative theorists of modernity who are now often lumped together by means of reference to 'multiple modernities', a term introduced by Shmuel N. Eisenstadt. This opposition, though, is rather unfruitful and the two subsequent chapters are meant to show ways in which it can be overcome.

Modernity as a set of institutions and its critique

From the early nineteenth century onwards, in works such as G.W.F. Hegel's *Elements of a philosophy of right* (1820), social theory and political philosophy worked with the assumption that contemporary Western societies had emerged from earlier social configurations by way of a profound rupture. This rupture, although it could stretch over long periods and occurred in different societies at different points in time, regularly brought about a new set of institutions, most importantly a market-based economy, a democratic polity and autonomous knowledge-producing institutions developing empirical-analytical sciences. Once such 'modern society' was established, a superior form of social organization was thought to have been reached that contained all it needed to adapt successfully to changing circumstances.

However, a considerable tension between any historical description of a rupture and conceptual understandings of modernity comes immediately to the fore. The conceptual imagery of the institutions of 'modern society' sits in an uneasy relation to historical dates. Were one to insist that the full set of those institutions needs to exist before a society can be called modern, socio-political modernity would be limited to a relatively small part of the globe during only a part of the twentieth century.

This tension between conceptuality and historicity was resolved by introducing an evolutionary logic into societal development. Based on the assumption of a societally effective voluntarism of human action, realms of social life were considered to have gradually separated from one another according to social functions. Religion, politics, the economy, the arts all emerged as separate spheres in a series of historical breaks – known as the scientific, industrial, democratic revolutions etc. – that follows a logics of differentiation (Parsons 1964; Alexander 1978). A sequence of otherwise contingent ruptures can thus be read as a history of progress, and the era of modernity emerges by an unfolding from very incomplete beginnings. In this view, indeed, modern society came to full fruition only in the US of the post-Second World War era, but 'modernization' processes were

25

moving towards that telos for a long time, and continued to do so in other parts of the world.

In conceptual terms, this perspective on modern social life aimed at combining an emphasis on free human action with the achievement of greater mastery over the natural and social world. The differentiation of functions and their separate institutionalization was seen as both enhancing human freedom and as increasing the range of action. Thus, the combination of freedom and reason, known from Enlightenment political philosophy, was transformed and, we may say, sociologized into terms such as subjectivity and rationality (e.g., Touraine 1992). Without this double concept being explicated in most of the theory of 'modern society', it nevertheless can be identified at the root of this conceptualization of modernity. At the same time, it certainly drew on what may be called the self-understanding of historical modernizers. Proponents of what came to be known as the scientific, industrial and democratic revolutions saw themselves acting in the name of freedom, and they also saw the new institutions they were calling for as providing greater benefits than the old ones.

After the dust of the great revolutions had settled, it became clear that the institutionalization of freedom and reason was a much less straightforward process than had been expected by Enlightenment optimists. As briefly mentioned at the outset, a series of major critical inquiries into the dynamics of modernity was elaborated successively from the middle of the nineteenth century up until the middle of the twentieth century. These critiques identified basic problems in the practices of modernity, but did not abandon the commitment to modernity as a consequence. They all problematized, although in very different ways, the tension between the unleashing of the modern dynamics of freedom and rational mastery, on the one hand, and its, often unintended, collective outcome in the form of major societal institutions.

The first of these critiques was the *critique of political economy* as developed mainly by Karl Marx. In contrast to some of the conservative critics of capitalism, such as the German historical economists who flatly denounced its rationalist individualism, Marx basically adhered to the Enlightenment tradition of individual autonomy. His ideal was 'the free association of free human beings.' In the workings of the 'free' market in capitalism, however, he discovered a societal effect of human economic interaction that asserted itself 'behind the backs' of the actors. In an economy based on market exchange and forced sale of labour power, relations between human beings would turn into relations between things, because they were mediated by commodities. Driven by laws of abstract value, markets would transform phenomena with a use value into commodities, the sole important criterion of which was the monetary value against which they could be exchanged. The result of such fetishization of products and money and of the reification of social relations would be the alienation of human beings from their work and its products, from other human beings and from themselves. In such an alienated condition, the possibility for autonomy and sovereignty of the economic actors would be completely eradicated, though these actors would indeed constantly reproduce these conditions by their own action.

The second grand critique was the *critique of large-scale organization and bureaucracy*, as analyzed most prominently by Robert Michels and Max Weber. With a view to the enhancement of rational mastery of the world, it postulated the tendency for the formation of stratified bodies with hierarchical chains of command and generalized, abstract rules of action. In the context of a universal-suffrage polity and welfare state, i.e. in 'large' societies in which all individuals had to be included on a formal, i.e. legally equal, basis in all major regulations, such 'dwellings made of steel' had emerged as state apparatuses, big industrial enterprises and mass parties and would spread further in all realms of social life. While such institutions in fact enhanced the reach of human action generally,

27

they limited it to the application of the rules, inside the dwellings so to say, at the same time.

In these terms, a variant of a critique of conceptions of rationality is the *critique of modern philosophy and science*, the third grand critique. Weber, too, was aware of the great loss that the 'disenchantment of the world' through rational domination entailed, still he understood his own social science in rational and value-neutral terms, as he thought no other approach could prevail under conditions of modernity. In contrast, radical and explicit critiques of science were put forward by others in very different forms. In idealist *Lebensphilosophie* the elaboration of a non-scientistic approach to science was attempted as well as, differently, in early twentieth-century 'Western' Marxism, i.e. by Theodor Adorno, Max Horkheimer and the early Frankfurt School. In some respects, pragmatism in the US can also be ranged under the critiques of science in as much as a new linkage of philosophy, anthropology and social science was proposed against the unfounded separation of spheres of knowledge in the disciplinary sciences. Such linkage would also bring the sciences back to a concern for the fundamental issues of the contemporary social world.

It was in pragmatism in particular – and in Europe in Durkheim's social theory – that a link between moral philosophy, social science and politics was maintained, or rather recreated with a view to responding to the contemporary problems of societal restructuring. This link gave rise to a fourth critique, the *critique of morality*. The problem may be schematically reconstructed as follows. The development of modern society entailed the risk of moral impoverishment, mainly due to two phenomena. The inevitable decline of unquestioned faith eroded a source that could provide foundations for moral behavior. And if recurring face-to-face interaction often is the basis for the solidarity-supporting insight in the human likeness of the other, such kind of interaction would be decreasingly relevant in mass societies integrated on the large scale of a nation. The two questions that arise are, first, how to ground ethics at all, when no foundational criteria are universally accepted, and, second, how to develop adequate standards for morality, when social relations are predominantly 'thin' and at the same time widely extended in space and time, that is, to relatively distant others (Boltanski 1993). The requirements for ethics have been raised, while the likelihood to agree on any ethics at all may have diminished, in such a view. Again, it is the achievement of reflexively questioning any imposed standards of morality that may subvert the possibility of any standard at all.

Synthetically, then, an argumentative figure emerged as follows. In the historical development of modernity as 'liberal' society, the self-produced emergence of overarching structures, such as capitalism and the market, organization and bureaucracy, modern philosophy and science, and the division of labour, is identified. These structures work on the individual subjects and their possibilities for self-realization – up to the threat of self-cancellation of modernity. The more generalized modern practices will become, the more they themselves may undermine the realizability of modernity as a historical project.

Modernity as experience and as interpretation

The interpretations of modernity provided by these critiques identified the tension between the modern orientations towards autonomy and towards mastery. They tended to resolve this tension in a clear-cut but also rather one-sided way, namely as the institutionalization of autonomy inevitably leading to forms of mastery that would subject the 'free' human beings. Alienation, atomization, commodification, bureaucratization and instrumental rationalization would assert themselves as absolutely dominant trends leading to the emergence of 'one-dimensional man' and 'one-dimensional society' (Herbert Marcuse). While this interpretation had some persuasive power, in particular during the first two thirds of the twentieth century, in its totalizing way of reasoning it underestimated the persistence of the ambivalence of modernity and the possible resurgence of

29

the quest for autonomy. Towards, the end of the twentieth century, socio-theoretical diagnosis of the present indeed shifted back to an emphasis on individualization, rather than atomization, and reflexivity, rather than rationality (e.g., Anthony Giddens, Ulrich Beck, Alain Touraine).

Although such recent analyses of modernity tend to employ the terminology of a new era (in response to the challenge of 'post-modernity' as discussed at the outset), they indeed draw implicitly on a different concept of modernity altogether. A common view of the history of social life in Europe holds that a 'culture of modernity' spread gradually over the past five centuries. This 'is a culture which is individualist [...]: it prizes autonomy; it gives an important place to self-exploration; and its visions of the good life involve personal commitment' (Taylor 1989, 305). Such an emphasis on individuality and individualization is quite alien to the totalizing critiques of modernity but also to the more formalized 'modern' discourses of the individual as in rational choice theory or in liberal political philosophy. And in the affirmative social theory of Parsonsian inspiration, the individual exists and indeed fully emerges only in modern times, but at the same time s/he is well integrated into norm-bound social life and appears 'deviant' when s/he transgresses those norms.

In European intellectual and cultural history, there has long been very little connection between the views of modernity and its inhabitants that praise agency and creativity of human beings, on the one side, and those that see the individual human being as either integrated in or submerged by social forces and structures. Given their interest in institutions and their stability, political philosophy and social theory proceeded predominantly by presupposition and showed little interest in actual human beings, who tend to be taken into account only as disturbances the more they enter the public scene. In literature and the arts, in contrast, the experience of modernity was in the center and, as experience, it concerned in the first place the singular human being and her/his creative potential (Berman 1982). Michel Foucault's lecture 'What is Enlightenment?' very succinctly distinguished between those two readings of modernity. Modernity attitude and experience demands the exploration of one's self, the task of separating out, 'from the contingency that has made us what we are, the possibility of no longer being, doing, or thinking what we are, do or think' (Foucault 1984, 46). It is opposed to modernity as an epoch and a set of institutions, which demands obedience to agreed-upon rules. At least in some writers, like Lyotard, the idea of post-modernity was inspired by such a return to what had been a modern self-understanding since at least the Enlightenment, and much less by the idea of a new era 'after' modernity.

Up to this point, we have identified a double opposition in the ways of theorizing modernity. First, those views that see modernity as the institutionalization of freedom and reason have been opposed by critics that see freedom being undermined by a legislating rationality. Second, both of these views have been criticized for failing to take into account the actual human experience of modernity and their variety. One of the outcomes of the post-1979 re-assessment of modernity stems directly from the analysis of this constellation: If the opposition of affirmative and critical analysis of modernity persists over long periods without resolution, this suggests that modernity is open to a variety of interpretations. And if both approaches tended to neglect experience, then the elaboration of a more comprehensive interpretative approach to modernity should proceed by exploring the variety of experiences of modernity.

Such an interpretative analysis of modernity has gradually been developed over the past two decades, and it starts out from the proposed reference to autonomy and mastery that seems to mark, even though the terminology varies, a commonality across all theories of modernity and thus a defining characteristics of modernity itself. Following Cornelius Castoriadis (1990; see also Arnason 1989; Wagner 1994), modernity can be considered as a situation in which the reference to autonomy and mastery provides for a double 'imaginary signification' of social life. By this term, Castoriadis refers to what more conventionally would be called a generally held belief or an 'interpretative pattern' (Arnason). More

31

precisely, the two components of this signification are the idea of the autonomy of the human being as the knowing and acting subject, on the one hand, and on the other, the idea of the rationality of the world, i.e. its principled intelligibility. Conceptually, therefore, modernity refers to a situation in which human beings do not accept any external guarantors – that is, guarantors that they do not themselves posit – of their knowledge, of their political orders or of their ways of satisfying their material needs.

Earlier social and political theory also recognized the modern commitment to autonomy and mastery, but it thought to derive a particular institutional structure from this double imaginary signification. Thus, it was often inclined to consider a historically specific interpretation of a problématique as a general trait of modernity. This is the case, for instance, when the historical form of the European nation-state is conflated with the solution to, as it was often called, the problem of social order, which was expressed in the concept 'society' (Smelser 1997, ch. 3). When assuming, however, that a modern set of institutions can be derived from the imaginary signification of modernity, it is overlooked that the two elements of this signification are ambivalent each one on its own and tension-ridden between them. Therefore, the recent rethinking takes such tensions to open an interpretative space that is consistent with a variety of institutional forms. The relation between autonomy and mastery institutes an interpretative space that is to be specifically filled in each socio-historic situation through struggles over the situation-grounded appropriate meaning. Theoretically, at least, there is always a plurality and diversity of interpretations of this space.

An interim summary may be useful at this point: The social and political theory of contemporary Western societies has long been based on the idea that those societies emerged through some rupture with the past. In this sense, scholars have long theorized 'modernity', as the attempt to grasp the specificity of the present, even though the term has been used only rather recently. The dominant strand has aimed at capturing this specificity by *structural-institutional analysis*. The modern institutions are here seen as the embodiments of the modern promise of freedom and reason. Against and beyond this dominant strand, three different conceptualizations of modernity have been proposed. First, the *critiques of modernity* have provided an alternative institutional analysis, emphasizing the undermining of the promise of autonomy in and through the workings of the modern institutions. Second, the *interpretative approach to modernity* has demonstrated the breadth of possible interpretations of what is commonly understood as the basic self-understanding, or imaginary signification, of modernity. Thirdly, the conception of *modernity as an ethos and an experience* has underlined the normative and agential features of modernity. In the former sense, it emphasizes the lack of any given foundations and the possibility to push the 'project of modernity' ever further. In the latter sense, it accentuates creativity and openness. In both ways, the experiential understanding complements the interpretative approach by underlining the large, potentially infinite, variety of interpretations of modernity.

Neo-modernization vs. the plurality of modernity

The theorem of multiple modernities, which has had the enormous merit of (re-) introducing the idea of a possible plurality of modes of socio-political organization into the analysis of 'modern societies', did not emerge directly out of the theoretical debate as it was sketched above, but rather from concerns of comparative-historical macro-sociology, that is, the study of large-scale social configurations and their transformations over time. Within that field, though, it addressed directly the problem that had been inherited from the theories of modernization of broadly Parsonsian inspiration, namely the assumption of long-term convergence towards a single model of 'modern society'. Significantly, the approach that is central to this opening, pioneered by Shmuel Eisenstadt (see, e.g., 2002, 2003), explained the persistent plurality through 'cultural programmes', thus introducing an interpretative approach, in methodological terms, and some idea similar to the 'imaginary signification' of society, in substantive terms. This approach has been widely received and recognized (see, e.g., *Daedalus* 1998, 2000; some contributions to Hedström and Wittrock 2009); however it has failed to make the strong innovative impact that one could have expected.

This – relative – failure is, among other reasons, due to two weaknesses of the multiple modernities approach: First, the strong idea of 'cultural programme' suggests considerable stability of any given form of modernity. Indeed, many contributors to the debate now reason in terms of civilizations, and 'classical' civilizations like the Chinese, Japanese or also the Indian one have been key objects for the identification of multiple modernities (see Arnason 2003 for the most nuanced contribution and chapter four below for further discussion). As a consequence, considerable limitations to the applicability of the approach are introduced, as it is difficult to conceive of South Africa, Brazil or even the USA or Australia in terms of deep-rooted, rather stable cultural programmes that merely unfold in the encounter with novel situations.

Second, the approach is based on only two main concepts: the characteristic (common and inevitable) features of modernity, on the one hand, and the (variety of) cultural programmes, on the other. This dichotomy limits the possibility of comparison since all difference between modernities needs to be explained in terms of the specific underlying programme.[1] In

---

[1] The only exception is (Northwest) European history, whose 'cultural programme' keeps being seen as generating 'original' modernity, and thus the problematic primacy of Europe in the analysis of modernity is inadvertently reintroduced (for a discussion of the relation between 'civilization' and 'modernity' see Arnason 2003, 34–51). Ibrahim Kaya's (2004) concept of 'later modernities', developed in an analysis of Turkish society since the Kemalist revolution, usefully points to a sense of crisis and need for change that may emerge in societies (or their elites) when comparing their own society with other ones that, for various and often partial reasons, are seen as superior or more advanced. Such approach overcomes the conceptual dichotomy by empirically investigating the interpretative resources that are mobilized within a given society and partly retrieved from outside that society.

this light, this approach either does not move far away from standard institutional analysis that permits surface cultural variation in terms of mores and customs or, alternatively, any supposed incomparability across cultural programmes raises the spectre of normative relativism, a key concern of political theorizing committed to modernity (to be addressed below in chapter three).

Indeed, the absence of a controversy between proponents of the multiple modernities concept and those who continue to work with a modernization approach, now sometimes referred to as neo-modernization to signal the reception of, and response to, earlier criticism, is striking. There is a profound opposition in at least two respects: the view of the dynamics of historical transformation, cultural resources on the one hand, a functional logic on the other; and the outcome of this dynamic, convergence towards a single institutional set-up on the one hand, persistent diversity on the other. Rather than giving rise to debate and exchange, though, this opposition seems to be seen as unresolvable by both sides and work concentrates on each side on the further elaboration of the own research programme (for a rare explicit confrontation see Schmidt 2010, heavily biased towards modernization theory though).

Both theoretical considerations and empirical findings have led the current author to side with an agency-oriented, interpretative understanding of modernity that makes the possible plurality of modern forms identifiable and analyzable. At the same time, however, too many deficiencies exist in the multiple modernities approach and too many valid issues are raised by modernization-oriented scholars to make the avoidance of communication a viable strategy. The concept of modernity has rightly been criticized as often being both too comprehensive and too imprecise to allow operationalization for research and clarifying communication in scholarly exchange (see Yack 1997). Thus, a most fruitful next step should be the disentangling of the concept with a view to separating out researchable aspects of modernity that can be compared across the dividing lines of recent scholarship. Furthermore, such dis-

entangling should be done with a view to making all contemporary societies amenable to analysis in terms of the specificities of their modernity
(or lack of it) under current global conditions, not only either Western
societies or their counterpart in the classical civilizations with their
apparently stable cultural programmes (details of such an agenda will be
spelt out in chapter four below).

3

Successive Modernities and the Idea of Progress

Major strands of socio-political thought have assumed that human societies pursue an evolutionary trajectory towards in some way higher forms of organization. In particular, it has been thought that the breakthrough towards 'modern society' in the course of the major social transformations of the late eighteenth and early nineteenth centuries marked the reaching of a superior state of history. The arguments varied. Political thought emphasized the commitment to individual autonomy and collective self-determination. Social thought identified the functional differentiation of society that permitted better satisfaction of current needs and higher adaptability to future needs. Critical thought identified flaws in the persisting class structure of modern society, but held that just one more revolutionary transformation would eliminate this last deficiency.

In their strong versions, these interpretations of recent human history as the march of progress have lost credibility. Not everyone was inclined to accept Jean-François Lyotard's claim that the end of all narratives of emancipation had been reached because they had been refuted by historical events. However, the evolutionist theories were now recognized as relying too heavily on assumptions from philosophy of history that could not in any way be 'tested' (using this term in a very broad sense) by historico-sociological research (see already Habermas 1981; and for a discussion Wagner 2001, ch. 5). In turn, the normative theories may in some way have established principles the validity of which one would not want to contest – the principles of freedom and equality being the prime examples. The questions, though, in how far these principles have been realized in existing societies and even if so, importantly, whether the form of their realization leaves the guiding ideas of those principles intact is often a matter of dispute.

Weaker versions of narratives of progress persist nevertheless. In sociological thought, simplistic theories of modernization prevailing during the 1950s and 1960s have largely been abandoned, but they have given way to neo-modernization theories that are less coherent but also more nuanced and the basic tenets of which are shared by many authors, even if sometimes implicitly. In normative political thought, few would deny that Jürgen Habermas makes a valid observation when he claims that the institutionalization of individual rights and of the rule of law marks an advance in human history, and even those critical theorists who raise objections would not discard the observation entirely but merely point to novel normative problems that arose in the aftermath and as a consequence of such institutionalization (see Karagiannis and Wagner 2009). The debate over the end of modernity and the rise of post-modernity during the 1980s and 1990s may not have had a clear conclusion, but by now one can see how the centre of discussion has shifted towards the exploration of forms of modernity rather than the end of it. Inadvertently (and sometimes one would want more explicitness), this means that the normative concerns of modernity and similarly the question where and how to identify their realization in the existing world have remained significant.

In this new light, the idea of plural forms of modernity has moved into the focus of attention. Sometimes it seems that this idea is by now widely accepted, but its implications are often unclear for a social theory and political philosophy that keeps normative concerns alive and aims to articulate them with socio-political analysis. It is often suspected that any embracing of the concept of plural modernities (under this or other names) necessarily entails the abandoning of normative concerns that ultimately are universal and unique, not plural and particular. In what follows I will first briefly return to the 'multiple modernities' debate as it originated in Shmuel N. Eisenstadt's work, but now concentrate on the concerns about relativism that the rise of this approach has raised from the view-point of normative theorists and will claim that these concerns – as is characteristic of debates over relativism – have not been conclusively addressed. Subsequently, I will shift terrain and discuss the plurality of modernity in analyses of transformations of modernity, 'successive modernities', as Johann Arnason called them.[2] Such historico-sociological analyses raise normative concerns about progress in a way that can possibly be more fruitfully addressed across the genre divide between historical sociology, on the one hand, and social and political theory, on the other, than the idea of multiple modernities, since the point of reference is 'the same modernity' that transforms in time through the structuring activities of its own members. The search for the dynamics of 'succession' under conditions of modernity leads to a re-assessment of the notions of crisis and critique and the link between them and thus also to a re-connection between history and normative philosophy via a discussion of the meaning of 'critique'. Such re-connection then needs to be elaborated in more detail, and this will done by using Axel Honneth's recent attempt at formulating a novel, empirically rich and historically situated theory of justice as the theoretical object against the backdrop of which a reconsideration of the idea of progress can take place with the insights from comparative-historical sociology in hand.

Multiple modernities and the spectre of relativism

As discussed above (in chapter two), the multiple modernities approach in its 'classic' version with a focus on civilizations works with some assumption of 'original' diversity, which is postulated and then used to

---

[2] The term 'successive modernities' was coined by Johann Arnason in his plenary lecture at the Congress of the International Institute of Sociology in Stockholm in 2005 and applied, among other authors, to my own work (Wagner 1994). The current article is an attempt to spell out what such 'succession' means and I hope I can be forgiven for using the occasion partly for an exercise in reflection about my own prior work.

explain contemporary and persistent plurality of modern socio-political constellations. In normative terms, such conceptualization of diversity is highly troubling. Let us for a moment assume – knowing well that such assumption has often been criticized – that Western-style modernity embodies some normative principles the adoption of which would mean progress. If so, which articulation of original cultural programmes would entail adoption of these principles and which one would not? In turn, if we assume that the original cultural programmes embody normative principles of potentially universalizable nature, what are the means to grasp what happens to them in the articulation with the arriving principles of Western-style modernity? Such questions are in the background of topical debates about, for instance, 'Asian values' or the 'Chinese road to modernity'. Theorists of multiple modernities normally do not claim that all modernities are equally modern. But they do not explore either along which normative lines modernities differ, thus leaving the question unasked whether the articulation of original cultural programmes with Western-style modernity is – or can be – progress. That is why normative theorists often see the spectre of relativism lurking behind terms such as plurality or multiplicity when applied to modernity.

In terms of comparative-historical sociology, the conclusions to be drawn from these deficiencies of the multiple modernities debate are fairly straightforward. For most current cases, first, the self-understanding of societies has not been stable for centuries but has undergone significant transformations, often even and especially in the recent past. Thus, there is no underlying cultural programme but rather an ongoing process of – more or less collective – interpretation of one's situation in the light of crucial experiences made in earlier situations. Second, rather than separating 'culture' from the institutional girders of modernity, one needs to demonstrate if and how re-interpretations of a society's self-understanding have an impact on institutional change, or in other words, how cultural-interpretative transformations are related to socio-political transformations (Sewell 2005).

Such steps should also go some way towards alleviating the concerns of normative theorists. As the starting-point of the analysis remains historical diversity, however, it will always be difficult to relate normative commitments generated within one context and identifiable there to normative commitments present in another context. One means to do so would be to use universal such commitments as a measuring rod, but it is not easily available. Philosophical debate has been, depending on what interpretation one prefers, either inconclusive in its work at discovering or creating universal normative claims or insufficiently concrete. In either case, the relation between an empirically identifiable normative claim and a universalizing formulation of an apparently similar claim may remain fuzzy.[3] For such reasons, we will here not explore the standard version of the multiple modernities debate further and just accept, for the purposes of this article, that the perplexities of normative theorists are understandable. The means to overcome them can more easily be created against the background of historico-sociological comparisons that do not start out from separateness and diversity.

Successive modernities: crises, critique and transformations of modernity

The theorem of successive modernities emerges from the study of a particular kind of major social transformations, namely those in which both the prior and the later state of the transforming social configuration can adequately be analyzed in terms of their modernity. This is a relatively novel claim because the functionalist theory of modern society had suggested that there would be no further major social transformation after a functionally differentiated institutional setting had emerged. Despite the

---

[3] I am not suggesting that this is always the case. If the constitution of a state denies one group of its population the right to political participation, as under apartheid conditions in South Africa, the commitment to equality is violated. The introduction of equal suffrage thus can without doubt be considered as progress in normative terms.

originally provocative nature of the claim to the contrary, enhanced by a vocabulary that suggested overcoming or superseding of some features of modernity in the course of the transformation (see above chapter two), the theorem of successive modernities is now widely accepted. It is applied, even though often not with great clarity, in numerous sociological studies of contemporary societies and recent tendencies of change. Its dominant version employs the idea of a transformation of modernity for a comparison of the current state of society with its state prior to, roughly, the 1960s, mostly assuming that this earlier state was well analyzed by sociological theorizing up to that point. This is the case, as briefly discussed above, for Ulrich Beck's (1986) distinction between a first, simple and another, second reflexive modernity, which has also influenced Anthony Giddens' (1990, 1994) considerations about institutional reflexivity as the novel feature of modernity. A similar imagery occurs in Zygmunt Bauman's (1987, 1989, 1991, 2000) writings about the legislating, order-producing, ambivalence-eliminating, solid features of (earlier) modernity that are contrasted with the interpreting, liquefying characteristics of more recent (post-) modernity. Alain Touraine's (1992) distinction between the subjectivizing and rationalizing features of modernity is more cautious in terms of periodization, but he, too, suggests that rationalization has long been the dominant aspect of existing modernity to be more recently being challenged by a newly rising concern with subjectivation. It should be noted that all these writings are underpinned by a normative agenda, but the evaluation of the two periods of modernity is, first, not the same across the authors and, second, not easily interpretable as progress or regress either. Rather, the authors point to novel challenges created by the transformation of modernity.

These analyses work with an overly simplified picture of the past modernity, taking the historicity of modern social configurations far too little into account. Aiming at more comparative-historical detail, my own reconstruction of the transforming modernities of West European national societies moved a crisis and transformation of European modernities towards the end of the nineteenth century into the center of attention, thus dividing the history of European modernities into three major periods rather than only two (Wagner 1994; see also Ewers and Nowotny 1986). Furthermore, inspired by Giddens' structuration theory, the analysis focussed on the experiences of modernity by the social actors themselves and on the interpretations they gave to those experiences rather than stipulating any actorless change in societal dynamics (as in Beck's case from functional differentiation to risky over-differentiation).

In this perspective, a social transformation is the outcome of a crisis of the earlier social configuration. Such crisis, in turn, is the perception of problems or shortcomings of the given practices in the light of principles, expectations or demands. The link between crisis and transformations is as follows (taking permission to quote myself):

> Practices have to be constantly reenacted to make them form institutions. If we see institutions as relatively stable sets of social conventions, then we may regard the building of such institutions as a process of conventionalization, and a crisis as marked by tendencies towards de-conventionalization, followed by the creation of new sets of conventions. The chains of interaction that link human beings may be reoriented or extended and the kinds of linkages that are used may be altered, and so societies change their shape and extension. Crises will then be understood as periods when individuals and groups change their social practices to such an extent that major social institutions and, with them, the prevailing configuration of institutions undergo a transformation (Wagner 1994, ch. 2).

Such transformations are not directionless; one modernity does not succeed arbitrarily to another one. Rather, a crisis of modernity is an event as a consequence of which societal developments are set on a different path (Wagner 1994, ch. 4). Despite the emphasis on individual and collective agency and problem-solving, though, normatively minded observers were not convinced that the opening of the analysis of modernity to the identification of a sequence of successive modernities would not abandon the whole question of modernity's normative commitments altogether (Habermas 1998).

This was a misunderstanding, but it was probably due to lack of explicitness in *A sociology of modernity*, even though some 'logics' in the history of (Western) modernity had been proposed. In brief: it suggested that this modernity was originally built on highly liberal but socially severely restricted principles. The consequences of these two features were inequality, impoverishment and exclusion, and criticism directed against those consequences demanded inclusion, equality and social security. These demands were largely satisfied by the transformation to the inclusive, bounded and organized modernity that came into being from the 1890s onwards and remained in place until the 1970s. But this transformation meant a strong standardization of practices and homogenization of life-courses as well as the reinforcement of external boundaries. By the 1960s, the direction of social criticism in Western societies began to change again, and the dismantling of the conventions of organized modernity meant extension of liberties and opening of boundaries (Wagner 1994, ch. 9). Luc Boltanski and Eve Chiapello (1999) developed a similar approach to analyze the transformations of French capitalism, which historically coincide roughly with the transformations of European modernity. They proposed the concepts of *'critique sociale'* and *'critique artiste'* to capture the different 'directions of criticism' and aimed to demonstrate how a particular capitalism is susceptible to provoke a particular critique and is then likely to transform in response to that critique.

Later work of my own developed this theme further. One study analyzed the French Revolution, the formation of the working class, the building of welfare institutions and the adoption of Keynesian demand management as partial transformations of European societies by means of re-interpretation of existing views of society, polity and economy in the face of situations regarded as problematic and in need of collective action (Wagner 2008, ch. 13). Another study read the history of European political philosophy from the idea of state sovereignty to totalitarianism in parallel to the history of European political modernity. It suggested that principles of political philosophy were created in response to problematic situations and were then available for use in later situations. Those later situations could differ significantly from the earlier ones, in which case conceptual amendment and further elaboration was required. Significantly, some problematic aspects of novel situations could be the consequence of the solutions adopted for earlier problems (Wagner 2008, ch. 10).

Intermediate observation on history and theory

Before these socio-historical analyses will be re-read in terms of the idea of progress that they convey (or not), the question of the relevance of historical analysis for normative theory needs to be addressed briefly. Philosophers are notorious for their difficulty in dealing with empirical observations unless the latter are constructed by themselves as exemplary cases to make a theoretical argument. Thus, so the often-heard argument, the empirical co-existence of a plurality of institutional arrangements that embody modern commitments has no relevance for a discussion of the universal nature of some modern normative principles. The claim underpinning this argument, which I otherwise fail to understand, must be that universalist reasoning cannot make itself dependent on empirical observation because it risks to succumb into particularity, that is, its risks falsification by reference to contradictory empirical evidence. In other words, universalist claims need to emerge from reasoning alone.

In my philosophically amateurish view, this position is untenable for three reasons. First, words are potentially meaningless outside of a context of application. Even abstract reasoning is abstracted from something, and while it may have internal linguistic coherence, cases of dispute will often need to be settled by returning to the concreteness from which had been abstracted. Second, all our politico-philosophical concepts have a context of origins, which often can even be uncovered and explored. Thus, they are historical. They can be moved far away from their origins, or they can be stretched to cover large 'spatio-temporal envelopes' (Bruno

Latour), but they remain historical nevertheless. Thirdly, validity is not necessarily affected by the inescapably historical, contextual nature of concepts. In particular the history of modernity can be considered as a history of stretching concepts to cover the entire globe. This may often have first occurred as a mere claim to validity, but some concepts, or some interpretations of some concepts, have indeed travelled far also in the sense of having been accepted as valid. Philosophical believers in universalism and progress should also believe in the possibility of human learning. Thus, the expansion of concepts to cover larger situations and be considered valid for them by more people can be one indicator – not the only one, though – for their general validity.

There is no need to make strong general claims here about the relation between history and theory. All that was needed was to preclude the objection that nothing can be gained for normative considerations from empirical comparative-historical sociology. History and theory do not dwell in different worlds.

Historical sociology and social and political theory (I): critique and the generation of progress

In this sense, returning to the main thread of reasoning, the critique that is at work in transforming modernity is always of a theoretical nature. Its immediate cause is a social situation seen as problematic. The problem, though, is rarely of an absolute nature. It becomes a problem when judged by a standard that is, one the one hand, available to the actors involved but, on the other, external to the situation itself, thus useable as a tool to measure the deficiency in the given situation (see Boltanski and Thévenot 1991). More particularly, in all cases analyzed in my own prior work, which focused on Europe, virtually all such criteria of judgement stem from the era of Enlightenment and Revolution. They often refer directly to the commitment for liberty and equality, and on other occasions in more complex ways to re-interpretations of the commitment to fraternity, very soon to be rephrased as solidarity (see, e.g., Sewell 1980). For nineteenth-century actors, the double nature of these commitments does not seem to cause any concern. They are clearly historical, as they refer to a not-too-distant historical experience. At the same, they already have a history of rapid diffusion and thus are endowed with general, potentially universal significance.[4]

Social change occurs in response to the critique and in view of solving the problem. Often, it is innovative, it creates novelty, even unprecedented novelty. The possible consequences of the novel solution, thus, cannot entirely be predicted. Two examples from the history of European modernity may illustrate the issue: First, the French Revolution inaugurated the novel political form of the republic based on popular sovereignty. Revolutionary optimists assumed that republicanism would spread quickly so that there would be no problem in building republics from the collective will of Europeans. Supportive but more sceptical observers (often German-speaking), in turn, suggested that some commonality of values and beliefs among the members of a collectivity committed to self-determination is required to make a republic viable. Such cultural-linguistic theory of the modern polity became the basis of national liberation movements, later nationalism and of the nation-state's policies of cultural homogenization. The theoretical argument is not flawed and not anti-modern either: it is committed to collective autonomy and defines the autonomous collectivity with a certain specificity. However, its proponents ignored or underestimated its possible negative consequences: that nationalism could become aggressive in a situation of competition between imperial states and economies; and that cultural homogenization policies could turn into both restrictions of individual autonomy and forms of exclusion.

Second, the liberation of market forces by granting commercial freedom, including the freedom to sell and buy labour-power, was based

---

[4] Reinhart Koselleck's *Kritik und Krise* (1959) remains of major importance for the emerging connection between principled critique and socio-political crisis in post-Enlightenment Europe.

on a whole series of normative arguments. The expansion of commerce would enhance domestic and international peace because of the mutual dependence on other human beings as producers of needed goods (the *doux commerce* argument). Specialization that results from production for a market rather than for own use would enhance productivity and thus increase the wealth of nations (the 'invisible hand' argument; see Hirschman 1977 for both arguments). And commercial freedom means the end of serfdom and of unjustified state imposition and is, therefore, itself a key expression of the modern commitment to individual autonomy. All of these arguments retain some validity. However, the experience with the application of such reasoning in the market revolution of the nineteenth century was impoverishment, rising inequality, decreasing quality of living and working conditions, and a whole series of collectivizing innovations were made to counteract the effects of the individualizing revolution towards economic modernity: recognition of trade unions, collective labour law, social-policy institutions, protective barriers to trade etc. (Polanyi 1944 remains an impressive account).

These two examples may suffice for the moment to elaborate an interim conclusion: there has been progress in the history of (European) modernity in the sense that socio-political problems have been identified and solved by recourse to action in line with modern normative commitments. In the direct, short-term comparison between two historical moments, there is often little doubt about achieved progress. Furthermore, such progress is not necessarily confined to short-term consequences. The end of serfdom and the introduction of freedom of commerce seemed so clearly demanded by the commitment to individual autonomy that juridical change in their direction led to the institutionalization of these freedoms as a means to safeguard normative achievements for future times.[5] However, there is

---

[5] An early observer of modernity expressed caution with regard to the possibility of securing accomplishments for the future: "Was Du geerbt von Deinen Vätern hast, erwirb es um es zu besitzen" (Goethe, *Faust*).

no guarantee of lasting, long-term progress as the – potentially negative, unforeseen and possibly unforeseeable – future consequences of the problem-solving action may be larger than the current positive effect of problem-solving. From this insight from historico-sociological inquiry, we now turn to historically sensitive normative philosophy to see how the same issue is addressed from that angle.

Historical sociology and social and political theory (II): progress in historically sensitive philosophy

The normative political philosophy of modernity takes the dual principle of individual and collective autonomy as its starting-point. There is some debate about the relation between the two aspects of the principle of autonomy (see Wagner 2008, chs 2 and 3, for a critical discussion), but much of political theory considers this principle as a universalist accomplishment derived from the ideas of liberty and equality that are seen as following directly from the step of recognizing other human beings as equally human (the assumption of 'common humanity', in Boltanski and Thévenot's terms). Recently, the attempt at building a universalist political theory has been enriched by adding a theory of justice that is built on no other principles than the afore-mentioned but nevertheless succeeds in universally grounding some commitment to redistribution of resources, or solidarity (Rawls 1971). The main objective of this approach was indeed to separate the variety of 'comprehensive world-views' that members of modern societies may hold from the collective normative commitments of their polity, which can be honoured by procedural means alone. The modernity of given societies and polities could then be measured by means of this yardstick.

Such theorizing has been criticized for mistaking historical developments in some Western societies for universal principles. In response, even defenders of the afore-mentioned principles have seen the need for 'historically situating' such proceduralist approach. This term has been used by Axel Honneth (2010) to refer to Habermas' analysis of contemporary modernity as grounded in the institutionalization of individual liberty through human rights and the rule of law in the liberal-democratic constitutional state. Honneth acknowledges Habermas' step towards historicization but criticizes the limitation to the liberal state as the sole institutional embodiment and defender of individual autonomy. In his view, elaborated at length earlier (Honneth 1992), human beings need recognition not merely in the legal sense, but also recognition for their contribution to the collectivity and recognition as a particular human being in private life. Thus, in addition to rights, human beings need love and respect.

For present purposes, Honneth's rich philosophy needs to be discussed only in two respects. In recent writings, first, Honneth emphasizes that love and respect, like rights, are needed for human beings to live autonomously. Rather than considering recognition as itself a basic need, it is seen as a prerequisite for individual autonomy. With this step, Honneth aligns his philosophy with broader strands of theorizing and turns it more explicitly into a philosophy of modernity – for this reason it becomes highly suitable here for discussing findings of the comparative-historical sociology of modernity. Second, Honneth suggests that the pluralization of spheres of recognition requires a more nuanced way of historical reconstruction than the mere reference to institutional accomplishments in Habermas's 'historically situated proceduralism'.[6]

---

[6] While I entirely agree with the step taken, the assessment of Habermas' work seems slightly unfair. After all, Habermas' most sociological theory of modernity, as contained in *Theory of communicative action*, combines institutional analysis (the distinction between systems and life-world and between economic and political-administrative systems) with reflections on social tendencies that upset or restore the balance between the spheres of society (the forms of colonization of the life-world and communicative action to reign in systemic overflow). Admittedly, there is little explicit history in Habermas' theory and he has not come back to it to, for instance, analyze commodification or juridification after the 1980s. But its explicit purpose was to assess progress and to criticize regress by means of substantive analyses of transformations of modernity, to use the language adopted in this article.

In Honneth's (2010) understanding, normative theory should no longer construct a neutral stand-point from which principles of justice can be identified and worked out, but rather reconstruct those principles from the historical processes of recognition in which they are always already effective as norms of mutual respect and consideration. Significantly, Honneth suggests that such theory can have 'confidence in historical reality' because the 'historically established relations of communication already contain', and 'socialised subjects are already guided by', the principles that the theory only has to explicate. This move is, on the one hand, an appropriate and necessary historicisation of the debate about normative principles; on the other hand, it shows a fairly optimistic view of history and of the subjects and relations of communication.[7] Indeed, Honneth sees the need to immediately add an 'exception': 'where social relations are ethically entirely destroyed and demoralized, a reconstructive theory of justice becomes helpless'.

The introduction of such 'exception' immediately raises the question how we identify normality. Or in broader terms, it suggests that even a reconstructive theory cannot entirely do without specifying basic criteria of normativity or, for that matter, without some concept of progress even after having abandoned the metaphysics of philosophy of history.[8] The utter absence of such criteria would then mark the exception; and under conditions of normality these criteria can serve as a 'measure' (very broadly understood) of progress or regress.

In related writings Honneth (in Fraser and Honneth 2003) has hinted at two such basic criteria, namely inclusion and individualization, with which the progress of recognition can be measured. The former seems rather straightforward. The more members of a given collectivity

---

[7] Precisely, Honneth speaks about 'more confidence' than proceduralist theorists, who need a suprahistorical stand-point to arrive at normative principles. In another respect, Honneth is more sceptical than proceduralists because he sees the possibility that abstractly developed principles may place overly high demands on social relations.

[8] As Honneth (2004) argues explicitly with regard to ways of interpreting Hegel's social theory.

benefit from recognition, and the more they benefit from all forms of recognition, the more inclusive is this collectivity and, by implication, the more it lives up to normative principles. The latter criterion is more complex. At first sight, it seems evidently applicable: if recognition enables individual human beings to live autonomously, then higher degrees of individualization should signal a state of social relations in which recognition is widespread. However, the term individualization is too ambiguous for such straightforward use. In the history of social and political thought it has certainly referred to increasing possibilities of self-realization; however, it has also been used for the uprooting of individuals from social settings with anomie, alienation, conformism and related phenomena as a consequence. As we shall see in conclusion, both criteria reveal more of their complexities in historical application.

Inclusion and individualization in European successive modernities
Have inclusion and individualization been the effects of social trans-formations in nineteenth- and twentieth-century (European) history? And if so, have these transformations had a normatively desirable effect that outweighs their possible negative consequences?

As briefly alluded to above, inclusion has been a key feature of European social transformations over the past two centuries. By 1800, only male property-owning heads of households were full citizens of modernity. Workers have found recognition as rights-holders and as contributors to the collective good through struggles from the 1830s to the 1970s. Women have found recognition as citizens between 1919 and the end of the Second World War; they have gained equal civil rights to men often only as late as the 1960s and 1970; and they have gained rights to their body through the legalisation of divorce and abortion that ended their being trapped by legal force in unwanted private relations that often lacked both love and respect. There has been progress through inclusion.

However, two further observations complicate the picture. The build-ing of inclusive, organized modernity from the late nineteenth century onwards was concomitant to the raising of walls between national societies through immigration restrictions, border controls etc. (see Noiriel 1991). Thus, processes of recognition inside national boundaries went with external exclusion and, thus, denial of access to recognition. Arguably, the two processes are connected: the granting of political and social citizenship was seen as requiring a definition and delimitation of the citizenry. In other words, internal recognition may go along with denial of external recognition raising the issue of justification of boundaries and of global justice and injustice. During the more recent transformation of organized modernity, in turn, novel forms of social exclusion (precarity) emerged after full juridical inclusion had been achieved and was maintained. There may thus be a connection between increased recognition of human beings as rights-holders, on the one hand, and, on the other hand, weakening of recognition of merit and solidarity – and maybe even of recognition in love and friendship when network capitalism erodes the boundary between work and private life (Boltanski and Chiapello 1999). Progress of inclusion in some respects has been accompanied by regress of inclusion in other respects.

Let us then turn to the question of individualization. The increase of individual autonomy has been a key commitment of European modernity from at least the sixteenth century onwards, even though it spread only gradually through society (Taylor 1989). From the early nineteenth century onwards, juridical change such as the formalization of individual rights following the Declaration of the Rights of Man and of the Citizen and the granting of commercial freedom gave a push to the orientation towards individual autonomy. Very soon, though, the negative consequences in terms of disembedding of human beings from their social contexts came to be felt. The subsequent long-term process of collectivization can only with difficulty be seen as further individualization. True, modern collective conventions and institutions include their members as individuals, but they do so by means of standardizing roles and homogenizing outlooks on the world. Tocqueville's insight that individualization may go along with increase of conformism was confirmed under organized modernity, at that time often called mass society. Unless we stretch the meaning of the term individualization so far as to almost mean the opposite of what Honneth has in mind, the period between the 1890s and the 1950s can hardly be seen as having brought progress of individualization. In turn, though, the post-1970s individualization may go along with new forms of exclusion, as mentioned above.

In sum, our brief application to the succession of modernities of criteria of progress as they emerge from normative philosophy tends to confirm the picture we have sketched above. We can identify historical progress in the transformations of modernity, and this should not come as a surprise as those transformations emerge from the articulation of critique and crisis in dealing with problematic developments within modernity. However, such progress in transformations does not constitute a long and linear line of normative improvement, as historical solutions to social problems may – and often do – cause novel normative deficiencies to emerge that are not necessarily of a minor nature compared to those that have been successfully overcome.[9]

---

[9] This suggests a return to the question of the 'exception' of a totally demoralized society, for which Honneth has situations such as Nazi totalitarianism in mind. It is problematic, however, to tear such situations outside of historical context. Nazism had its conditions of emergence in earlier German and European developments, and during its rise it was seen by many as a solution to problems of liberal restricted modernity. The radical decay of normative standards in historical reality cannot be dealt with by a change of approach and a sudden reliance on 'moral reasoning alone' (Hegel as referred to by Honneth) – or only at the cost of failing to understand the possibility of such decay and thus making its return more likely (see Lefort 1999).

4

Trajectories of Modernity: Comparing European and non-European Varieties

The preceding two chapters analysed the plurality of modernity and the conditions for normative progress in modernity in the light of recent debates and findings. The next step to take is to apply the insights from these explorations to the comparative study of modernities and their historical trajectories to see in more detail how modernities differ and where they make progress, or not, in the realization of modernity's normative principles. This chapter aims to develop a conceptual and empirical programme to accomplish this task. To do so, it first will reflect on the 'unit of analysis', that is, to explore in which we way the concept of modernity can be attached to collectivities of human beings.

The destructuring of social theory and the rise of civilizational analysis
Until the late 1960s, structuralism and structural-functionalism, and the accompanying sociological theory of modernisation, had provided objectivist pictures of society that rested on the idea of strong ties between human beings guaranteeing coherence and a stable socio-political order. The conceptual elements varied between the approaches, but some combination of an interest-based, an identity-based or an institution-based explanation, emphasising structure and social class, system and function, culture and nation, and procedure, law and state respectively, was always at play. The analysis of entire socio-political configurations, then generally referred to as 'societies', did not appear to pose any major conceptual or empirical problem.

In the area of sociological theory, this thinking was challenged in all respects during the 1970s and 1980s. To give just some key examples: Anthony Giddens's work stands for the turn away from functionalism; Pierre Bourdieu's for the opening up of the structuralist tradition towards considerations of issues of temporality and agency; and Jürgen Habermas and Alain Touraine have tried to diagnose contemporary Western societies without entirely fixing their institutional structures in any modernised version of a philosophy of history. In addition, empirical findings proliferated on subjects as diverse as personal identity and selfhood, forms of political participation or technologies and organisational forms of production, which all undermined the image of a generally stable and well-ordered society which had prevailed in the sociology of the 1950s and early 1960s. These theoretical and empirical developments have led to a situation in which many of the established categories of sociology have been challenged by a justified and irrefutable critique. In one sense, it seems as if contemporary modernity requires a new sociology for its analysis. In another sense, though, 'modernity' may itself look like one of those overly presupposition-rich concepts that can no longer be sustained, at least not as a term capturing the basic features of an entire social configuration (see Yack 1997).

In some strands of debate, the postulation of 'collective concepts' (Max Weber) without sufficient investigation of the social phenomena they referred to became the explicit target of criticism. This line of criticism recently ushered into emphasising ideas of increased 'individuality' and tendencies towards 'individualisation' in contemporary social life. The emergence and assertion of the individual as a being without predetermined strong connections to or within collectivities has moved to the centre of sociological interest. Together with the parallel debate on 'globalisation', a sociological image of the contemporary world has emerged in which there are no social phenomena 'between' the singular human being, on the one end, and structures of global extension, on the other. The concomitant rise of an individualist-atomist ontology, most explicitly in rational-choice theories, makes it difficult to even conceive of social phenomena other than aggregations of individual acts. The view of globalisation as an unstoppable and uncontrollable dynamics, as also largely in Anthony Giddens' metaphor of the 'juggernaut', underestimates the significance of its human-made character, thus its being amenable to re-interpretation and change. And the displacement of the idea of radical change from the collectivity and its history to the singular human being and her/his 'bare life' (Giorgio Agamben) completes the new image of a world in which social relations may have global extensions, but are so thin and ephemeral that contemporary modern human beings are held to realize their own lives in a social context that they cannot conceive of as their own. As the earth becomes entirely subjected to human intervention, the world, in the sense of the social space that human beings inhabit, recedes into unrecognizability – a situation Hannah Arendt had described as 'worldlessness'.

This is an image of contemporary modernity that at best captures some recent tendencies in the restructuring of social relations; it can hardly be upheld as the basis for a renewed sociology of contemporary social configurations. If it were valid as the characterisation of inescapable trends, then the social world would become devoid of social structures as well as of forms of domination. It would be inhabited by individual human beings pursuing their lives by constantly reshaping their orientations, achieving what they achieve on the basis of their abilities alone, and moving in an open social space which itself would be constantly adjusting in line with the evolving orientations of the human beings that populate it.

This imagery refers to observable transformations but conceptualises them in such a way that their current force is exaggerated and their future continuation held to be inescapable. Importantly, the current image works with the extreme end-points of social life, the globe and the human body, and thus conceptualises away any structured existence of 'the social'. Historically, sociology has always refused to accept any imagery of this kind. It elaborated and insisted on an understanding of 'the social' as that which is in-between singular human beings, precedes their interpretations of the world and is amenable to re-interpretations. For some period and for some authors, true, the concept of 'society' suggested that such 'social' had an eternal form – or had found its lasting form in 'modern society'.

This was an error from which sociology has started to awake. It now needs to take up its historical agenda of analysing and understanding the major transformations of the social, and it needs to do so with regard to the current such transformations, without accepting the ideological prejudice that those transformations spell the very end of this agenda.

In response to this challenge, some authors, and among them most notably and most subtly Johann Arnason, have revived the concept of 'civilization'. Noting the link between the concepts of civilization and culture, Arnason (2003, 1–2) neatly captures both the specificity of civilizational analysis and the two key dimensions any such analysis needs to address: 'interpretations of culture can focus on comprehensive forms of social life as well as on the constitutive patterns of meaning which make such forms durable and distinctive'. In other words, civilizational analysis deals with interpretations and meanings and it asks to which degree such interpretations are deeply *shared by a collectivity* so that they provide the basis of forms of life, and to which degree they are patterned so that they become *continuous over extended stretches of time*. Historically, civilizational analysis has mostly presupposed highly affirmative responses to both the questions about commonality and continuity. The current re-reading in a pluralist light, such as Arnason's, turns such presuppositions into questions for analysis, even though arguably some considerable commonality and continuity needs to exist to speak of a civilization.

The following reflections are meant to explore how far such a concept of civilization can reach in analyzing the contemporary global social constellation. More specifically, it will raise some doubts about the ability of even pluralist civilizational analysis, and the associated multiple modernities approach, to fully open up to empirically observable lack of identity over time and less than comprehensive grip of patterns of meaning on the members of a collectivity. The reasoning will proceed in four steps. First, a brief review of the recent conceptual debate in social theory and historical sociology will lead to the conclusion that concepts such as 'civilization' and 'modernity' still work with too strong presuppositions about continuity and commonality and need disentangling. Second, a proposal will be made to distinguish several basic problématiqes that all human collectivities need to address and to suggest that such distinction lends itself to research-oriented disentangling of various aspects of social phenomena. In an explorative manner, thirdly, this approach will be applied to South Africa and Brazil, two social configurations that can fruitfully be studied as collectivities but lend themselves much less to civilizational analysis. By way of conclusion, fourthly, the trajectories of these non-European modernities will briefly be compared to the European one to illustrate the potential of this approach for a global sociology of plural trajectories of modernity.

Continuity and commonality in the transformations of the social: From multiple modernities to societal self-understandings

The approach proposed here joins in with developments in social theory and historical macro-sociology such as the return to human agency in the so-called 'structure-agency debate' of the 1980s (with Giddens 1984 as the main reference-point here); the overcoming of evolutionist approaches and the critique of unfounded use of 'collective concepts' (Max Weber; most important here Mann 1986); and the more recent elaboration of theories of social change that emphasize collective creativity and the re-interpretative, cultural component in every major social transformation (Sewell 2005).

Turning away from any idea of evolution as differentiation, theories of the constitution of societies see the formation of patterned social life not as the result of a meta-historical logic but as the work of human action and creativity. The terminology goes back to Anthony Giddens' path-breaking volume *The constitution of society* (1984), which suggests a theory of 'structuration' of society that fully takes agentiality and historicity into account. Giddens offered a compelling critique of functionalism as a social theory that starts with a concept of 'society' and suggests a logic of evolution of societies in terms of functional differentiation that proves unsustainable on both theoretical and historical grounds. Alternatively, he suggested that any society is constituted through the practices of its living members who are, in principle, capable of altering through creative agency any 'social structure' that they inherited from the preceding generation. Proponents of differentiation theory, whether of a strictly functionalist or of a 'softer' kind, have never been able to convincingly respond to the critique by Giddens and other authors who participated in the return to agency in social theory. Giddens, unfortunately, never followed up on his own programme for a social theory of long-term transformations, but other, more historically inclined sociologists have taken up the issue and have tried to apply versions of structuration theory to the historical analysis of social configurations. For present purposes, the works by Michael Mann and William Sewell are particularly noteworthy.

In his *Sources of social power* (2 vols., 1986, 1993), Mann provides an impressive long-term analysis of power 'from its beginnings' to the early twentieth century. He proposes an approach focused on networks of variable forms of power that may have different spatial extension and different durability and, accordingly, rejects any notion of 'society' because it makes too many presuppositions about the coherence of social practices. He addresses the specificity of Europe, a theme central to sociological debate at least since Weber, in terms of the emergence of a 'European dynamic' after the crowning of Charlemagne as Emperor by the Pope in 800 CE. Significantly, Mann sees this event as a rupture that creates a novel trajectory, thus ruling out all possibility of considering the Roman Republic and Empire as the 'seedbed' (Talcott Parsons) of European modernity.

Mann offers a concise and innovative general conceptual proposal and then 'applies' it in lengthy analyses of historical developments. Particularly visible now in the collection of essays *Logics of history: social theory and social transformations* (2005), William Sewell, in contrast, focuses on a more fine-tuned conceptual elaboration that has evolved from selective historico-sociological analysis, in particular on the history of the French

Revolution and its long nineteenth-century aftermath. For instance, he analyzes the interactions between the Parisian population, the National Assembly in Versailles, and the French king in the days before and after 14 July 1789 to see how 'the French Revolution' was created from an open sequence of local actions and interpretations. We retain here specifically the notions of an 'event' as a structure-transforming occurrence and of 'collective creativity' as frequently a key ingredient that turns an occurrence into an event in the afore-mentioned sense.

The juxtaposition of Mann's and Sewell's works as cornerstones for rebuilding a historically sensitive social theory shows that considerable problems remain. Sewell acknowledges that his approach, as elaborated thus far, will tend to favour relatively small-scale occurrences whose larger and long-term implications can be convincingly shown, as his analysis of the storming of the Bastille demonstrates, but whose analysis does not yet amount to an investigation of long-term developments as such. Thus, his work does not enable us to answer the question whether a common pattern of meaning, which we could call 'European civilization', pre-existed the French Revolution and provided resources for its possibility. Nor can we conclude from his work that the structure-transforming event of the storming of the Bastille marks the birth of modernity as a rupture with any preceding comprehensive form of social life. For the analysis of such long-term trajectories, Sewell merely points to Mann's work as an example that such an extension of his own approach is possible. Looking at Mann from this angle, in turn, it becomes evident that the conceptually guided description of long-term developments tends to lead to an imagery of multi-faceted, entangled processes of network expansion and contraction in which it becomes difficult to answer sharply posed questions about continuities and commonalities.

The problem thus is: The most persuasive work at the interface of social theory and comparative-historical sociology gives us little leeway to answer the question whether there is in human history such long-term continuity and large-scale commonality that suggests the use of the concept 'civilization'. Does this imply that we need to 'drop' the question, to use one of Richard Rorty's favourite metaphors (e.g., Rorty 1989), to consider it as one of the concerns of the philosophy of history that now have been overcome because we have no means to address them? The following considerations are motivated by the insight that such 'dropping' is no solution. Methodological obstacles need to be overcome wherever there is reason to assume that some commonality and continuity exist, however difficult it may be to trace them in detail. There just may sometimes be social phenomena of large size and relatively stable long-term duration for which one cannot easily say how they, or some of their features, persist across large spatio-temporal envelopes.

Towards this end, the elaboration of a concept of 'societal self-under-standing' is proposed here. Such concept permits to take distance both from the traditional view that 'social structures' directly determine human action and cause social change, on the one hand, and the more recently arising view that all social phenomena can be explained by means of the aggregation of the rational actions of individuals, on the other. The very usefulness of the concept of 'society' has been an issue of debate within sociology (from Alain Touraine to Michael Mann; most recently Outhwaite 2005). The criticism is based on both grounds of empirical observation and theoretical reasoning. On the one hand, recent social change is said to have led to the dissolution of the coherence of national societies in economic, cultural and political respects; on the other hand, theoretical reflection has tended to deny the validity of Durkheim's proposition to see 'society' as a reality *sui generis* above and beyond human motivations and actions. Valid as both of these observations are, it remains nevertheless true that human beings have endowed themselves with the capacity to collectively act upon their ways of living together and that a purely juridico-political concept such as the state does not capture the manifold ways in which such action is possible. Rather than abandoning the concept of 'society', the task is to re-conceptualize it beyond notions such as 'national character', 'people's spirit' or 'collective identity', the more time-honoured ones of which had already been effectively criticized by Max Weber (Wagner 2010). The concept of 'self-understanding' provides such a more tenable underpinning of 'society'. Rather than on high commonality among its members or on socio-structural cohesion, it focuses on communication between human beings about the basic rules and resources they share, and on the sedimented results of such communication. As such, it draws on the idea of societal 'mise en forme', implicit in Tocqueville and actualized by Claude Lefort (1986) and relates to Cornelius Castoriadis's (1975; Arnason 1989) concept of 'imaginary signification of society', recently popularized by Charles Taylor (2005).

Against the background of the deficiencies of the multiple modernities debate (as sketched above in chapter two) and by implication much of 'civilizational analsis', the requirements for innovation in the comparative sociology of contemporary societies and their historical trajectories stand out clearly: For most current cases, *first*, the self-understanding of societies has not been stable for centuries but has undergone significant transformations, often even and especially in the recent past. Thus, there is no underlying cultural programme but rather an ongoing process of – more or less collective – interpretation of one's situation in the light of crucial experiences made in earlier situations (see Wagner 1994 and chapter three above). *Second*, rather than separating 'culture' from the institutional girders of modernity, one needs to demonstrate if and how re-interpretations of a society's self-understanding have an impact on institutional change, or in other words, how cultural-interpretative transformations are related to socio-political transformations (Sewell 2005; see Raaflaub 2011 for a similar analysis of the emergence of democracy in ancient Greece).

In some recent scholarship, these two steps have been taken. However, the impact of these innovations is still limited, mostly due to two reasons: first, the identification both of societal self-understandings and of their articulation with institutional forms still poses problems for research, despite important steps towards operationalization of concepts (see the following section); and second, there are inherent difficulties of substantively rich – i.e. not merely indicator-based – comparisons of large societies with rather different historical trajectories (to be discussed subsequently).

The basic problématiques of human social life: towards a novel comparative sociology of trajectories of modernity

The main challenge for an interpretative-institutional comparative sociology is the analysis of societal self-understandings and their transformations in such a way that comparability between societies becomes possible. Self-understandings may – and will tend to – refer to aspects and events that are specific to a given society, such as the moment of foundation – e.g., the (contested) idea of the birth of the United States out of the spirit of Lockean individualism (Hartz 1955) – or a highly significant collective experience – e.g., the (recently debated) self-understanding of the Italian Republic in the light of the *Resistenza* against fascism and occupation. These notions, valid as they may (or may not) be, do not lend themselves directly to comparison with other societies, or if so only on a far too general level.

In response to such important objection, it is suggested to abstract from those identifiable self-understandings those elements that concern a *limited set of basic problématiques* that all human societies need to address. In earlier work, we proposed a set of questions: (a) as to what certain knowledge a societal self-understanding is seen to rest upon; (b) as to how to determine and organize the rules for the life in common; and (c) as to how to satisfy the basic material needs for societal reproduction, and referred to these questions as the epistemic, the political, and the economic problématique respectively (Wagner 2008; for a related attempt at disentangling, see Domingues 2006). To say that a society embraces a *modern* self-understanding, furthermore, implies that all these questions are truly open; that answers to them are not externally given but need to be found; and that, therefore, contestation of the validity of existing answers is always possible.

The distinction of these problématiques marks a *first step* towards the disentangling of societal features that then can be systematically compared. In brief: the fact that societies need to effectively address these problématiques by searching for their own answers is what is *common* among all 'modernities'; the fact that the questions are open to interpretation; that there is not any one answer that is clearly superior to all others (even though one answer can certainly be better than others and societies will search for the better ones and/or those that are more appropriate to them; see above chapter three) and, thus, that several answers can legitimately and usefully be given constitutes the *possible plurality* of modernity.

In a *second step*, the *range of possible answers* can be further identified in a relatively general and abstract way by scrutinizing the history of epistemological, political and economic thought – even though one will need to be aware of the risk of Eurocentrism if such reconstruction stays close to the currently established canon. In a very synthetic way, the following key issues emerge:

The epistemic problématique interrogates first of all the degree of certainty of knowledge human beings can attain with regard to themselves, to their social life, and to nature. Translating this issue into socio-political matters, it further raises the question to which degree such knowledge can or should be used to determine socio-political issues. Given that answers to both of the preceding questions can be contested under conditions of modernity, thirdly, one needs to ask in how far claims to certain knowledge – in comprehensive world-views – can be made collectively binding in any given society. This last question directly links the epistemic to the political problématique. The central issue of the latter concerns the relation between those matters that should/need to be dealt with in common and those others that should/can be left to individual self-determination. Modernity's basic commitment to autonomy leaves the relation between individual autonomy (freedom from constraint, or freedom from domination) and collective autonomy (democracy) rather widely open to interpretation. Despite occasional claims to the contrary, modern political theory has not provided a single and unique answer; thus, there is a plurality of interpretations. More specifically, the political problématique also concerns the extension and mode of participation in political decision-making (the question of citizenship) as well as the mode of aggregation in the process of collective will-formation (the question of representation). The centre of the economic problématique is the question as to how to best satisfy human material needs, and it can be alternatively answered in terms of productive efficiency and in terms of congruence with societal values and norms. Among the latter, the commitment to individual freedom may rank highly in which case freedom of commerce will be considered an, at least partially, appropriate institutional solution. But other values – including value-based responses to the epistemic or political problématiques – can complement, or compete with, the value of individual freedom, in which case other answers are required (the classic, path-setting study is Polanyi 1944; see now Joerges et al. 2005).

In all its brevity, this account should have demonstrated: that there is a plurality of possible ways of responding to these basic problématiques, even under conditions of modernity (against a key assumption of much social and political theory culminating in the works of – as different as these authors are – Talcott Parsons, John Rawls and Jürgen Habermas); that, further to their internal openness to contestation and interpretation, the responses to these problématiques can be articulated in different ways; that the need to articulate individual and collective autonomy is a thread common to all problématiques, and it is central to the political one.

Based on such disentangling of the concept of 'modern societal self-understandings', it is also possible to operationalize the analysis of major societal transformations, that is, introduce a historical, dynamic perspective into the analysis of, indeed, trajectories of modernity. Such transformations, and this is the *third step* of operationalization, will now be identified in terms of either changes in the responses given to a single problématique or in the articulation between problématiques or both. Given the increase in specificity, compared to the more general concept 'self-understanding', such changes can often also be directly related to institutional change, such as, for example, constitutional change in the relation between church and state, or the forms of embeddedness of market self-regulation.

In historical analysis, such transformations can be traced to 'events' (William Sewell) in which actors respond to experiences they have made through re-interpretation of their understandings of the basic problématiques. Often, such an event will be the experience of failure of an established response to one or more of those problématiques. The re-interpretation will aim at providing a superior answer through the mobilization of the available cultural resources. This mobilization entails collective creativity; thus there is no cultural or civilizational determination (even though there may be path-dependency). In turn, there is no guarantee for lasting superiority of the new answer, as any new response may generate new fault-lines; thus, any view of societal 'evolution' as necessarily entailing learning processes that lead to higher levels of human social organization is equally flawed (see above chapter three).

The current plurality of global modernity: postcolonial situations and the characteristics of the South African and Brazilian trajectories

The recent research on plural forms of modern socio-political organization has had a particular empirical focus on settings that lend themselves more to civilizational analysis than others, to be explained against the basic assumptions held and methodologies preferred. Thus, considerable work has been done on the 'classic' civilizational areas, such as China, Japan and India. There is also relevant work on predominantly Islamic societies, but this work is strongly pre-determined by the questions whether modernity and Islam are compatible, in a culturalist vein or critical thereof, or what the obstacles to development in those societies are, in a neo-modernist vein. In all of these cases, the – *prima facie* plausible – assumption of radical cultural diversity between these regions and the alleged 'original' modernity of the West works so strongly in favour of culturalist or neo-modernist approaches – the choice often depending more on the scholar than on the findings – that breakthroughs towards novel understandings of current global modernity are practically impossible at the current state of debate, despite all the merits of many of the existing studies. An important exception here is scholarship in cultural studies, in which, however, problématiques of modern self-understandings often tend to be dissolved into processes of 'glocalization' or 'hybridization', losing out of sight the valid questions that stood behind 'Eurocentric' conceptual frames that underpinned colonial domination (as analyzed by Chakrabarty 2000).

In contrast, the question of the specificity of modernity cannot be avoided in all cases of the 'founding of new societies', to use the formula that Louis Hartz (1964) employed for the analysis of societies in which groups of colonial settlers interacted with native populations, in obviously highly asymmetric ways, in the institution of new societies. While the colonial period mostly goes back to the 16th and 17th centuries, the actual founding of societies often occurred at the turn from the 18th to the 19th century in conjunction with the Enlightenment and the French Revolution and sometimes in conscious application of social contract theories. Thus, there is no doubt about the modernity of such newly founded, indeed first post-colonial societies in terms of commitment to collective self-determination. At the same time, the terms of the contract, so to say, often deviated considerably from the European or French understandings, in the light of the particular situation in those societies, and the 'contracts' kept undergoing changes in the face of further experiences made (e.g., Beilharz 2008; Lake 2008). In other words, postcolonial societies of this kind are, on the one hand, clearly analyzable in terms of their ways of handling the modern problématiques, but on the other, they have embarked on historical trajectories that vary considerably from the European one.

Among the 'new societies' of this kind, only the US has been the object of sustained scholarly debate about 'self-understandings', to a significant degree taking off from Louis Hartz's earlier – and much better known – work, the identification of individualist liberalism as the societal self-understanding of the US (Hartz 1955). This analysis has been widely debated and, at some distance, been opposed by, first, an insistence on the republican tradition in the American self-understanding (Pocock 1975) and, second, by the identification of a plural communitarianism on a liberal background (Walzer 2001) as the twentieth-century self-understanding of the US. Significantly, these responses to Hartz, as important as their contribution to political theory has been, have largely ignored both the native population of North America and the African-Americans as forced settlers and have thus provided a very partial view of the American self-understanding. In this sense, they fall behind the much earlier study of 'the American dilemma' in which Gunnar Myrdal (1944) aimed at analyzing what was then known as 'the Negro question' in terms of an 'American creed' (as a remedy see now Henningsen 2009).

The strong interest in the North American self-understanding is related to the long dominant position of the US in world politics; and its particular expression needs to be understood against the background of the almost accomplished extinction of native Americans and the dominated position of African-Americans, who as the most sizable minority in the US are predominantly of lower class and thus have had considerable difficulties in making their voices heard. Weak scholarly interest in other 'new societies', with the exception of area specialists, needs to be explained in a different way. These societies were too dominated by the European settler groups to find strong interest in postcolonial studies, which have focused on South Asia (the most innovative one being Chakrabarty 2000) and, to some extent, on de-colonized African societies. In turn, they have been analyzed by modernization theorists mostly because of their 'delays' in modernization that was in need of explanation – this holds in particular for Latin American societies that looked sufficiently 'Western' to raise developmentalist expections but then fell short of fulfilling them. Or alternatively, Marx-inspired analyses, often from within these societies, developed critiques of modernization theory, but without elaborating new angles on modernity. In the perspective developed here, in contrast, it is precisely for the reason of this ambiguous position that the study of 'new societies' can generate not only novel insights about the trajectories of these societies but also trigger conceptual innovation in social and political theory and in comparative historical and political sociology.

South Africa and Brazil are particularly suitable choices for an innovative analysis of the plural trajectories of modernity as they share some features that support an analysis in the proposed terms:[10] First, both societies show particularly pronounced and complex relations between the various population groups, a fact that has enhanced the need of these groups to consciously reflect on their own societal self-understanding. Second, both societies have initially adopted rather specific political forms, addressing the particularity of their colonial experiences in terms of both the external relation to the 'mother country' (or countries, in the case of South Africa) and the internal relations between the population groups. Thirdly, both societies have responded to further experiences through post-colonial transformative re-interpretations of their initial self-understanding and by developing a conscious self-understanding or even 'project' of their own particular modernity. Fourthly, in both societies,

---

[10] From this point onwards, this section reports from a project in the process of elaboration that aims at providing a broad re-assessment of existing research on those 'new societies' by re-reading it under the angle of societal self-understandings. It will focus in particular on South Africa and Brazil including in-depth studies of their historical trajectories and current interpretations of modernity (The project is funded by the European Research Council under grant no. 249438). For this reason, we will now further concretize the approach by discussing, in a very preliminary way that will still be subject to verification in the project itself, some main features of these societies.

the most recent phase of fully inclusive democracy showed features of a particularly pronounced societal reflexivity (epitomized by the Brazilian transformations leading up to the Porto Alegre World Social Forum in the one case, and by the Truth and Reconciliation Commission in the other), having had strong repercussions in global debate. But, fifthly, both societies also show extremely high social inequality and face the urgency to address this situation, not least in the face of widespread violence and crime. And finally, both societies experienced considerable industrial development and have, at times, consciously deployed economic-policy strategies, placing them firmly as important actors in the current global context.

At the same time, there are numerous fundamental differences between South Africa and Brazil, and as in the case of the similarities, these are differences that lend themselves to comparatively elucidate the conditions for the formation of societal self-understandings. We can identify some general aspects and then further differentiate according to the ways in which the basic problématiques are addressed. The general aspects concern the early tie to the mother country and the kind of 'colonial encounter' (Asad 1995) between the population groups.

Brazil emerged from a conscious, state-driven colonization project and had long remained subordinated to Portugal, whereas the first Europeans settled in South Africa to support long-distance trade without a colonization project, and the settlers, in particular the first group of Dutch origin, who became the Afrikaner, soon developed an early new collective identity, disconnected from their origins (Thompson 1964). Brazilian colonization originated, as most other cases, as the settlement of one group of Europeans on territory inhabited by a native population. The situation changed drastically when for economic reasons large numbers of Africans were re-settled and forced to live and work as slaves, creating a society composed of members of three distinct origins. While the latter also holds for South Africa in general terms, this society witnessed originally a highly conflictual relation between two European settler groups, the Dutch and the British. In particular the former fought the native population in frontier zones, but both groups otherwise relied on dominated Africans for domestic or farm work and services. In South Africa, too, economic development, in this case gold and diamond mining, altered the relation between groups, as the industrial work of large numbers of Africans transformed domestic subservience into class relations.

In this context, we can discern some key elements of the – rather highly different – ways in which the basic problématiques were addressed:

The epistemic problématique: As a statist project, Brazil 'inherited' Christianity as its official religion from Portugal, and in particular a version of Neo-Thomism as a social and political philosophy that started out from a kind of social contract but emphasized order and hierarchy, while at the same time allowing for pragmatic arrangement in everyday situations (Morse 1964: 153–8). As a planned intervention, Christian colonization embarked on a debate about the nature of the native populations and integrated them, in principle, into the Christian understanding of humanity. Thus, (religious) knowledge resources were employed to guide social and political action on the basis of a concept of humanity that embraced hierarchy without strong boundaries. From the late 19th century onwards, the expectation for superior knowledge guiding societal developments was translocated to the sciences, particularly the comprehensive approaches in the social sciences (Schwartzman 1991).

In contrast, there was no common project, and no pronounced higher-knowledge base either in South African colonization, which was economically founded – initially in commercial terms, then in terms of agricultural subsistence for the first colonists. The relations to the African population were dominated by military control and economic exploitation, without much further concern about 'the other' (even though there was some Christian-Calvinist justification of principled inequality). With growing interdependence of the groups due to industrialization, and in particular with the downward social mobility of the Afrikaner group after the South African War, the weakness of the epistemic basis of social life became problematic. A 'scientific' theory supporting the 'racial' segregation that already existed, and even demanding the formal separation that became known as apartheid, was developed with a marked contribution by sociology, in particular by Afrikaner authors (Jubber 2007; Coetzee 1991).

The political problématique: As independent states, Brazil emerged in the form of a constitutional monarchy in 1822 and was transformed into a republic in 1889, and the Union of South Africa in 1910 was the result of the unification of several polities of highly different composition and rule within the British Commonwealth. While the former, in terms of citizenship regime, can at first sight be regarded as pursuing the gradual path towards ever more inclusive democratization not unlike European societies, the latter witnessed increasingly entrenched segregation along with massive denial of rights, including political rights, in particular to the African population. Prior to the return to democracy after a military regime in Brazil and to the end of apartheid in South Africa, the political class in both societies had developed particular mechanisms of 'inclusion' and 'representation': the mass union-centred corporatism in Brazil and the rule through leaders of the segregated groups and 'states' in South Africa. This mechanism came to a radical end with the introduction of equal universal suffrage in South Africa, a major political rupture in this society, and it has become increasingly inoperative in Brazil due to the weakening of the unions in the recent neo-liberal phase of capitalism and the emergence of 'insurgent citizenship' (Holston 2008) in the urban centres of Brazil. In both cases, recent changes have created novel kinds of political problems, for which new solutions are being sought, often by adapting the former model, but are clearly not yet found (Domingues 2008; Larrain 2000). Significantly, though, we may witness in these societies the transformation of 'low-intensity democracy', which was long considered functionally adequate also for Europe and the US, towards more participatory forms of democracy.

The economic problématique: The economic situation of both Brazil and South Africa is marked by availability of resources and thus actual and potential wealth, but also by export-dependency and by weak redistribution policies, thus high social inequality. In both cases, as mentioned above, the societal significance of the 'racial' question increased for economic reasons because of slave import in Brazil and internal migration of Africans towards production sites in South Africa. Only in South Africa, though, a horizontally stratified system of largely endogamous classes emerged due to segregation, whereas 'inter-ethnic' relations have been much more widespread in Brazil with more loose correspondence of skin colour to social class – as well as an official disinterest in this question. Both societies aimed to move towards greater self-sufficiency, in Brazil in the form of import substitution policies inspired by dependency theories, in South Africa in response to the – always incomplete – isolation imposed by sanctions against the apartheid regime, but both have also revised these policies more recently (Domingues 2008).

In both societies, the elites – composed and defined in highly different ways – have long practiced a societal organization that depended economically on a majority of the population that was not enfranchised in terms of citizenship. Lack of formal juridico-political citizenship persisted in South Africa until the end of apartheid; in Brazil, formal criteria for dividing the population being historically less pronounced and today absent, the exclusion from political citizenship gradually ceased to exist, but exclusion from social citizenship remains strong. In both cases, the key challenge resides in radically transforming the old model of societal organization. From this brief, conceptually driven account, though, it should already have become clear that meeting this challenge is not 'merely' a matter of a new economic profile (Salais and

Storper 1993) and stronger socio-economic redistribution. What seems to be required – and what is being actively searched for in both societies – is a new arrangement of modernity that includes novel forms of (social and political) knowledge as well as novel understandings of citizenship, participation and representation – thus, new answers to the epistemic and political problématiques, too (see Santos 2006–07).

Comparing non-European and European varieties of modernity

After this brief sketch, it is possible to indicate the contours of the comparison between non-European and European trajectories of modernity with a view to opening a perspective on plural forms of modernity that emphasizes interpretation of patterns of meaning without relying on a concept of civilization that seems to be too fraught with historical and theoretical burdens to be fruitful today.

It is part of the 'classic' European self-understanding that polities are in control of their territory and are built by, and on the foundation of, homogeneous populations. These are basic assumptions behind the concepts of, first, state sovereignty and, then, popular sovereignty (even though federalism should not be underestimated as an alternative option long fallen in oblivion). The idea of homogeneity could be expressed alternatively or complementarily in civic, cultural, linguistic, or ethnic terms, but in each case this assumption both alleviated and guided the search for answers to the *political problématique*. The subsequent problems of citizenship and representation were addressed through mostly slow and gradual extension up to equal universal suffrage in the former case (often reached only by 1919, in some cases after the Second World War), and through social cleavage-based formation of political parties in the latter.

The *economic problématique* was 'modernized' in Europe by the idea that extension of the commercial bonds between human beings would either pacify societies or maximize their wealth or both. This thinking inspired the market revolution from the late 18th century onwards. Experience with market self-regulation, however, solicited re-interpretations of this idea, which were put forward in a great variety of ways from the second half of the 19th century onwards and all entailed some kind of non-market organization of national economies. These novel responses did not only re-articulate the economic and political problématiques, in terms of creating the 'states versus markets' debate, they also entailed the inclusion of the working classes (and sometimes the female population) into the polity, as the period of economic 're-regulation' coincided with the period of extension of citizenship.

Both the original and the revised interpretations of the political and the economic problématiques drew on resources provided by the ways of handling the *epistemic problématique*. In the 17th century, European modernity referred to natural rights as a basic orientation. The dissolution of the old regimes, which could no longer be justified, however, created high contingency and radical uncertainty, in response to which new kinds of knowledge were produced, in particular theories about the social bond that sustained some notions of likely order even under conditions of self-determination. The theories of the commercial bond were mentioned above; theories of the cultural-linguistic bond sustained efforts to solving 'the national question' and creating homogeneity; and theories of social interest-based bonds, solidaristic as in Durkheim or antagonistic as in Marx, pushed towards solving 'the social question'. Significantly, the interwar years of the 20th century saw 'collective existentialisms' emerge from both the 'national' and the 'social' debates, underpinning the rise of totalitarianisms.

It was only in the post-Second World War period that the radical interpretations had been defeated and were withdrawn or moderated in Western Europe. The new polities worked with some compromise of liberal, national and social ideas and hoped to bind those ideas together with a more technocratic version of social science as an epistemic reference-point. Many observers agree that this model entered a new crisis with new needs for re-interpretation. Debates about neoliberalism, globalization or individualization are indicators of the dissolution of the model, but, as discussed at the outset of this chapter, they do not indicate directions for new responses, not least because they underestimate the role for collective agency and creativity (Karagiannis and Wagner 2007). At this point, the trajectories of South Africa and Brazil meet with the one of Europe. In the former societies, rather radical transformations are ongoing, whereas in Europe the predominant – and far from insignificant – response is regional integration, often pursued in the hope that more radical re-interpretations can be avoided. The European re-interpretations proceed from a position of superior power in the global context, but not necessarily from a position of richer cultural-interpretative resources at hand to find new answers. Precisely because crucial questions such as those of internal homogeneity or of accomplished social inclusion were considered closed and stabilized in Europe, the European social imaginary may have difficulties in re-opening those issues and finding novel solutions. A truly global sociology of modernities will need to consider Europe a particular case among others, not least to be able to retrieve all the resources that might be needed for arriving at novel solutions that are at least temporarily superior to the old ones.

Like civilizational analysis, this sociology focuses on interpretation as the human way to give form to their world; and like Johann Arnason's approach to civilizations and the multiple modernities debate, it finds persistent plurality of such interpretations even – or: in particular – under current conditions of so-called globalization. As the examples of Brazil, South Africa and Europe should have shown, however, such interpretations are often more contested, more dynamic over time, and less tightly bound to a given collectivity than even a pluralist concept of civilization suggests. Thus, we propose to introduce the concept 'societal self-understanding' to overcome some of the problematic connotations of the concept of 'civilization' and see civilizations as a particular form of societal self-understanding that is highly continuous over time, rather well tied to a given collectivity, and so deeply rooted that it undergoes little contestation at its core. Some such civilizations may exist, but many currently living human beings do not form part of them.

5

Towards a World Sociology of Modernity

Sociologically, modernity – and more recently 'globalization' – have often been described in terms of time-space compression (most explicitly Harvey 1990). Without giving particular theoretical or definitional significance to this term, it is undoubtedly fruitful to connect the experience of modernity to human ways of situating their own lives in time – in its most basic sense, to be modern means to be in one's own time – and extending their relations to others in space.[11] As my preceding reflections are a programme rather than a result, they will not be followed by conclusions in the usual sense of the term but rather by some brief, sometimes manifesto-style observations of how an investigation of the contemporary condition of modernity would need to situate the modern experience in time and space.

Space (1): multiple modernities and our relation to the axial age

It is understandable but rather unfortunate that the theorem of multiple modernities addresses the current plurality of modern forms of socio-political organization by resorting to the claim of a long-lasting parallel unfolding of different cultural programmes (see above chapter two for some detail). The objective of arguing for persistent plurality is thus achieved, but the historical origins of the claim tend to fall into oblivion. After all, Shmuel Eisenstadt's analysis is grounded on a reconsideration of the so-called axial age, the period between roughly 700 and 400 BCE, around which, so the original philosophical version, world history turns, separating pre-history from history. However one judges the current state of the axial age debate (see Arnason et al. 2005 for a comprehensive

---

[11] Reinhart Koselleck's (1979) felicitous characterization of the change in European political languages between 1770 and 1830 as distancing the horizon of expectations from the space of experience expresses a temporal statement in a spatial metaphor.

re-assessment), the hypothesis does not only claim that parallel and somewhat similar major socio-cultural transformations occurred in several regions of Eurasia during that period, it also needs to affirm some, even though thin, interconnectedness between those regions, as otherwise the parallelism would be a highly unlikely coincidence. Thus, a more adequate version of the multiple modernity theorem would place less emphasis on the separate and different origins of various cultural programmes and consequently some fundamental diversity between contemporary modernities and would focus instead on the long-term interconnections in world history that not only permit historico-sociological comparison but also suggest that there may be some proximity, or family resemblance, between the basic problématiques that human beings tried to address collectively at various places and points in time.[12]

Time (1): from the ancients to the moderns

In a most general sense, and keeping the limits of our knowledge in mind, the axial-age transformations can be seen as a period of profound self-questioning and as the conscious introduction of new ways of interpreting the world at a moment of crisis (Wagner 2005). It is not common parlance to refer to the social configurations that emerged from these transformations as modern, with the partial exception of Athenian democracy, but it is worthwhile to reflect more on their modernity, with all its limits, and in particular on the modernity of the transformations themselves.

The idea of any strong and direct connection between the axial-age social configurations and those of our present era cannot be sustained. No one does so for the relation between Greek democracy or the Roman Republic and present Europe, and thus Western thinkers should be cautious in suggesting any such continuity for other 'civilizations', such

---

[12] Bearing in mind that such proximity of problématiques does not warrant a return to the idea of universal perennial problems for which straightforward conceptual solutions are to be sought, rightly criticized by Quentin Skinner (1969).

as the Chinese one, which may emerge only due to the ignorance about finer details of Chinese history. On the other hand, the alternative assumption of radical discontinuity, as promoted for instance by Aldo Schiavone (1996), only begs further questions. Even if we allow for radical re-interpretations, we need to account for the facts that our socio-political language derives many of its key concepts from ancient Greek and that Continental European juridical institutions operate on the basis of canonized rules that are known as Roman Law. In other words, a long historical perspective on the history of modernity should centrally focus on the question of the relation between 'the ancients and the moderns' as neither one of straight continuity nor of radical discontinuity. Those authors who contributed to formulating that distinction, such as Benjamin Constant, were after all not drawing a sharp line of separation but were investigating degrees of difference and similarity (see Karagiannis and Wagner forthcoming).

Space (2): 1800 – European modernity or modern world-making?

The years around 1800 are often considered as the period of the origins of European modernity. Unlike some postcolonial authors and critics of Eurocentrism, I do not see any need to deny or downplay the crucial impact of European developments during this period on socio-cultural transformations worldwide. This is very different from saying, though, that modernity began in Europe and then diffused across the world. The latter argument is normally sustained by one of three explanations, or a combination of them, that require a brief review.

First, the diffusion of modernity has been explained by theorists of modernization and development as triggered by the performative superiority of a functionally differentiated society. In Talcott Parsons' own writings (see, e.g., Parsons 1964), however, the argument is presented in a less forceful way than his followers often assumed. Drawing on the analogy with natural selection, Parsons leaves considerable space for 'survival' of a variety of 'species' due to insulation or identification of 'niches'. Introducing more recent ecological concerns, one can go further and suggest that diversity is an asset in its own right given greater probability of adaptation in changed circumstances. But we should not carry the analogy too far, as social change in human societies is reasonably seen as quite distinct from natural selection. Staying closer to historical evidence, we can recognize that elites in some societies perceived European developments across the nineteenth century as a challenge to which they needed to respond (see Kaya 2004). This is the case for the Russian and the Ottoman empires in both of which a debate about the need for, and the degree of, 'Westernization' emerged. Towards the end of the nineteenth century, related debates emerged in China and Japan, though the degree of confidence in one's 'own' institutions and culture was higher than in the afore-mentioned cases. The outcome of these 'encounters' (to use again Talal Asad's term) arguably altered the trajectory of the non-European societies, but it is not fruitfully to be seen as either Westernization or the assertion of a long-standing cultural programme but rather as a selective perception, active interpretation and modified introduction of certain features of 'European modernity' in the given context.

Second, the need for adaptation because of European military superiority might be seen as a special case of the perceived higher performance of the West. It is a very special case, however, because the encounter is here determined by the risk of military defeat and possibly extinction, not by any feature of the West that is regarded as worthy of emulation in its own right. The European colonizers had without doubt the higher 'firing power' and many colonial encounters were determined by this difference. The history of South Africa provides a good illustration as neither the Dutch nor the British settlers were initially aiming for colonization in the more narrow sense of the term, that is, occupation of the territory and domination over the local population. The Dutch settlers invaded the territory further only when exposed to stronger British settlement and domination in the coastal trading-posts, and even then their encounters with the native African population was limited to those parts of the territory that they occupied for agricultural purposes. The African societies resisted for considerable time successfully, and historians do not detect any economic superiority of the colonizers that determined the outcome of the encounters. Western occupation and the subsequent destruction or transformation of African societies was determined by military power (Thompson 2000).

Finally, the diffusion of European modernity can be seen as due to the normative attractiveness of the principles of individual and collective self-determination. Under the long reign of more materialist explanations of history, including modernization theory, during the latter half of the twentieth century, such views were rarely heard, but they are coming more strongly to the fore nowadays that the language of 'human rights and democracy' returned to the core of the contemporary self-understanding. Indeed, many occurrences in the late eighteenth and nineteenth centuries can be interpreted in this light as assertions of the principle of collective self-determination, most significantly in the Americas with first the American and Haitian declarations of independence and subsequently the creation of independent states in South America. Such 'founding of new societies'(Hartz 1964) against the background of earlier colonization was clearly inspired by the modern imaginary as it had been developed in Europe, but again we cannot speak of a case of simple diffusion. The newly founded societies displayed a breadth of interpretations of modernity that again needs to be understood by the encounter of already different European 'fragments', to use Hartz's term, with different native populations. Current studies of varieties of such non-European modernities can build on the presence of the modern imaginary from those founding moments onwards and will then need to reconstruct the subsequent historical trajectories as re-interpretations of the form of that imaginary adopted at the outset (see, e.g., Larrain 2007).

In sum, the moment of 1800 is in global perspective not the beginning of the diffusion of European modernity, but rather the onset of parallel processes of world-making, inspired by the modern imaginary but pursued under conditions of considerable power differentials.

Time (2): 1880s-1960s – a global organized modernity

The particularity of the United States of America resides in the fact that their foundations are rather symmetrically erected on both individual and collective autonomy. The latter principle strongly informed all founding of new societies as a move towards independence from the colonial powers, but the commitment to, and interpretation of, the principle of individual autonomy varied highly, both in terms of its inclusiveness and the distinction between economic and political liberties. Since oppression on grounds of religion was a major reason for the early North American settlers to leave Britain, the commitment to religious freedom became a corner-stone of the self-understanding of the United States as a society committed to the freedom of individual expression, as lastingly confirmed in the Bill of Rights added to the US Constitution. Elsewhere, in Europe and in many new societies, the liberal modern imaginary informed political debates in a pivotal manner but hardly ever reigned supreme for extended periods before 1970s.

In Europe, as described in more detail elsewhere (Wagner 1994; see also chapter three above), the liberal imaginary was first restricted by means of exclusion of large strata of the population, in a formal way by means of limits to civic rights and political participation, in more informal ways through limited access to 'modern' economic and cultural practices. As the imaginary provided the resources for the transcendence of those 'original' limitations, a major line of internal critique of modernity demanded full inclusion. Such inclusion was by and large accomplished by the first inter-war period by means of organizing modernity around collective concepts such as most importantly nation and class, at the expense however of channelling the expressions of individual liberty into the containers of large-scale organizations, as 'secondary' means of containing the reach of the modern imaginary.

Looking beyond Europe, we can recognize how colonial domination became the global concomitant to the 'original' restrictions of liberal modernity. In analogy to eighteenth- and nineteenth-century views of women and workers, European property-owning male thinkers clearly recognized that special justifications were required to exclude groups of human beings from modernity once the latter's imaginary was accepted, and a variable mix of biological, socio-structural and historical reasons were invoked to explain why Africans, in particular, were not able to shoulder the responsibility that goes along with the recognition of their full autonomy. An educational view of the relation between the Europeans and the colonized was created employing parental, domestic concepts of responsibility for beings who, though human, were still in a state of minority. In parallel, European action towards the colonized was seen in terms of efficient intervention towards 'development' following an industrial model of mastery and control. Such discourse prevailed until the 1970s in European development-policy documents, that is, far into the era of decolonisation in the name of collective self-determination (Karagiannis 2004).

The South African situation showed a partial exception that overall, though, confirms the domestic-industrial approach towards non-European others. The apartheid conception of separation and domination, later referred to as 'separate development', was gradually elaborated during the first half of the twentieth century to find full institutional expression in the regime that came to power in 1948. Thus, the era of apartheid coincides with the period of organized modernity, including a contestation-ridden build-up up to the Second World War and the full elaboration in the second post-war era. In the place of a detailed analysis, an example may here suffice: The District Six Museum in Cape Town documents the social destruction of an inner-city neighbourhood when apartheid rules were used to impose the relocation of the population of highly mixed ethnic origins and religious beliefs in favour of the building of a 'whites only' quarter. One display in the exhibition, at first sight surprisingly, shows urban planning policies in the Swedish city of Malmö during the 1960s, without further comment – and without need for any since the thought-provoking power of this display in its context works on its own.

Time (3): 1970s-2010 – globalisation as the destructuring of organized modernity

Contemporary South African society struggles to overcome the apartheid heritage. Social inequality and residential segregation are not easily removed even by a majority party that is firmly in power and has an efficient state apparatus at its disposal for policies of transformation. Furthermore, apartheid is part of the lived experience of the 'coloured' and 'black' population of South Africa that cannot be negated or denied without the risk of depriving experiences and the memory of them of any reasonable significance. Jacob Dlamini's *Native nostalgia* (2009) analyses life in a township under apartheid by recalling it to memory, including his own. Such memory is not without fondness, and the – liberal-democratic – present does by far not always compare favourably with a past marked by oppression and exclusion. In this respect, it resonates with European or North American nostalgic longings for the orderly world of the 1950s and 1960s that withered away in the face of individualization and globalisation, as current sociological and journalistic jargon has it.[13]

We may just note here, pending deeper analysis, that European organized modernity faced gradual de-conventionalization from the late 1960s onwards that ended in a more or less negotiated collapse of a partial world order between 1989/1992 and maybe 2010, if the current

---

[13] In some respects, the book may be compared with Edgar Reitz' monumental film *Heimat*, evoking German everyday life under Nazism and during the 'restorative' early second post-war period.

financial turmoil will turn out to have the deep institutional impact that some observers now expect. Described in this way, European history during the past half century looks less dissimilar from the South African one than we are used to.

Space (3): the global present – rethinking freedom, equality and solidarity

The preceding observations should have suggested that, 'globalization' being far from an entirely novel phenomenon, we have lived in a highly common world for two and a half centuries, even though we have interpreted it in a rather large variety of ways at different times and different places. Sociologically, the transformations of this world should be analysed in terms of changing structures and extensions of social relations – authoritative, allocative and ideational ones (Wagner 2010) – and the preceding analysis should have given some ideas and concepts as to how this – enormously difficult – task can be addressed and possibly accomplished. Such analysis, even if pursued in a flawless way, will gain its full significance only if it is set into the context of the modes of normative philosophy that have accompanied modernity with great explicitness over the past two and a half centuries and in a more implicit or indirect way over much longer periods. Here three brief remarks in terms of a reappraisal of the normative commitments of the French Revolution have to suffice.

It may be true, first, that individual liberty has never had such a prominent place in world history as it has now. Major theoretical efforts have been made to separate – liberate, some may want to say – the idea of individual freedom from conceptual contexts that were seen as endangering its full meaning. Time and again, however, it has also been observed that such attempts have had the opposite effect: by abstracting freedom, to paraphrase Hegel's terminology, from the practical contexts in which free action only can be meaningful some conceptual purification was possibly be achieved but at the price of losing all significance and relevance (Wagner 2008, chs 2 and 11). 'Globalization' spells the weakening of meaning-providing contexts, and as such it may create new spaces for 'individualization'. But such apparent normative gain, to return to Honneth's criteria of progress (above chapter three), may occur against the background of the weakening of inclusion-providing institutions and their accompanying modes of recognition.

The inclusion-providing institutions of organized modernity, namely, operated – and arguably needed to operate – with clear and strong boundaries of eligibility or membership. Organized modernity showed some achievements in terms of domestic justice and equality, but it had no means to address the global situation beyond the boundaries of a given state. To phrase the issue of equality and justice in a slightly provocative way, second, we may ask under which conditions a theory of 'separate development', the justificatory pillar of the apartheid regime, is justifiable. The separate organization of modern nations in the name of self-determination is not as far away from 'separate development' as defenders of modernity are inclined to think. The nation-state model was built implicitly on the assumption that those states were equal and were also equally providers of justice to their members. In practice, though, this was clearly often not the case. Inside nation-states, the relations between the English and the Scottish, or between North and South Italians, were relations of inequality and domination. Between nation-states, this was similarly the case between, for instance, Sweden and Finland, or Great Britain and Portugal or Argentina.

We have to recognize that normative 'separation' is justifiable at best in the pronounced absence – or thinness, to use a common metaphor – of economic, political and cultural ties between the members of the respective entities. Whenever there are significant such ties, considerations of justice need to cross the boundaries of these entities. Coming back to the example, the apartheid notion of 'separate development' was at most somewhat defendable before gold and diamond mining drew large numbers of black Africans into the economy and society of the dominant white groups – and this means before any such ideas were even formulated. Once such hierarchical division of labour on highly unequal terms had emerged and consolidated, no justification of separateness was defendable any longer. In turn, we have to ask whether the current global division of labour has not created a density of economic ties across the world that requires the urgent development of concepts and practices of global justice (see Ypi 2008 for a constructive proposal).

Such latter development will need to be underpinned by a novel understanding of the ties that make human beings commit themselves to consider the fate and destiny of other human beings. Re-interpreting older understandings that referred to such ties as friendship, pity or brotherhood, the early nineteenth-century socio-cultural transformations in Europe witnessed the emergence of the novel term 'solidarity' for which soon claims of superiority over the older terms emerged. Solidarity was supposedly built on equality not paternalistic hierarchy; on abstraction not proximity; and on reason not passion. Despite those claims, though, the term found its transposition into concrete historical forms in concretised versions of national solidarity and class solidarity as well as its institutional translation into the welfare state. Thus, it came to refer too closely to the social configuration of organized modernity to be of unmodified use in the global present. The current destructuring of organized modernity requires anew a 're-specification of the social bond with a political view' of the kind that was achieved during the nineteenth century but capable of creating and maintaining world in the face of the current risk of worldlessness (the above draws strongly on Karagiannis 2007 from which the quote stems).

References

Alexander, Jeffrey C., 'Formal and substantive voluntarism in the work of Talcott Parsons: A theoretical and ideological reinterpretation', *American Sociological Review*, 43, 1978, 177–198.

Arendt, Hannah, *The human condition*, Chicago: The University of Chicago Press, 1958.

Arnason Johann P., 'The imaginary constitution of modernity', in *Autonomie et autotransformation de la société. La philosophie militante de Cornelius Castoriadis*, Giovanni Busino et al., Geneva: Droz, 1989, 323–337.

Arnason, Johann P., *Civilizations in dispute*, Leiden: Brill, 2003.

Arnason, Johann P., Shmuel Eisenstadt and Björn Wittrock, eds., *Axial civilizations and world history*, Leiden: Brill Publishers, 2005.

Asad, Talal, *Anthropology and the colonial encounter*, New York: Prometheus, 1995

Beilharz, Peter, 'Australian Settlements', *Thesis Eleven* 2008, no. 95: 58–67.

Bauman, Zygmunt, *Legislators and interpreters*, Cambridge: Polity, 1987.

Bauman, Zygmunt, *Liquid modernity*, Cambridge: Polity, 2000.

Bauman, Zygmunt, *Modernity and ambivalence*, Cambridge: Polity, 1991.

Bauman, Zygmunt, *Modernity and the Holocaust*, Cambridge: Polity, 1989.

Beck, Ulrich, *Risikogesellschaft*, Frankfurt/M: Suhrkamp, 1986

Berman, Marshall, *All that is solid melts into air. The experience of modernity*. New York: Simon and Schuster, 1982.

Boltanski, Luc, and Eve Chiapello, *Le nouvel esprit du capitalisme*, Paris: Gallimard, 1999

Boltanski, Luc, and Laurent Thévenot, *De la justification*, Paris: Gallimard, 1991

Boltanski, Luc, *La souffrance à distance*. Paris: Métailié, 1993.

Castoriadis, Cornelius, *Le monde morcelé. Les carrefours du labyrinthe III*. Paris: Seuil, 1990.

Castoriadis, Cornelius, *The imaginary institution of society*, Cambridge, MA: MIT Press, 1975.

Chakrabarty, Dipesh, *Provincializing Europe: postcolonial thought and historical difference*, Princeton UP, 2000.

Coetzee, J. M., 'The Mind of Apartheid: Geoffrey Cronjé (1907–)', *Social Dynamics* 1991, vol. 17, no. 1: 1–35.

Daedalus, 'Early modernities', vol. 127, 1998, no. 3, summer.

Daedalus, 'Multiple modernities', vol. 129, 2000, no. 1, winter.

Dlamini, Jacob, *Native nostalgia*, Johannesburg: Jacana: 2009.

Domingues, José Mauricio, *Latin America and contemporary modernity: a sociological interpretation*, London: Routledge, 2008.

Domingues, José Mauricio, *Modernity reconstructed*, Cardiff: University of Wales Press, 2006.

Eisenstadt, Shmuel Noah, *Comparative Civilizations and Multiple Modernities*, Leiden: Brill, 2003.

Eisenstadt, Shmuel Noah, *Multiple modernities*, Piscataway, NJ: Transaction, 2002.

Ewers, Adalbert, und Helga Nowotny, *Über den Umgang mit Unsicherheit*, Frankfurt/M. Suhrkamp, 1986.

Foucault, Michel, 'What is Enlightenment?' in *The Foucault Reader*, ed. by Paul Rabinow. London: Penguin, 1984, 32–50.

Fraser, Nancy, and Axel Honneth, *Redistribution or recognition? A political-philosophical exchange*, London: Verso, 2003.

Giddens, Anthony, 'Living in a post-traditional society', in Ulrich Beck, Scott Lash and Anthony Giddens, *Reflexive modernization*, London: Sage 1994.

Giddens, Anthony, *The consequences of modernity*, Cambridge: Polity, 1990.

Giddens, Anthony, *The constitution of society*, Cambridge: Polity, 1984.

Habermas, Jürgen, *Die postnationale Konstellation*, Frankfurt/M. Suhrkamp, 1998.

Habermas, Jürgen, *Der philosophische Diskurs der Moderne*, Frankfurt/M: Suhrkamp, 1985.

Habermas, Jürgen, *Theorie des kommunikativen Handelns*, Frankfurt/M: Suhrkamp, 1981

Hartz, Louis, *The founding of new societies: studies in the history of the United States, Latin America, South Africa, Canada, and Australia*, San Diego: Harcourt, Brace, Jovanovich, 1964.

Hartz, Louis, *The liberal tradition in America, An interpretation of American political thought*, New York: Harcourt, Brace, Jovanovich, 1955.

Harvey, David, *The condition of post-modernity*, Cambridge: Blackwell, 1990.

Hedström, Peter, and Björn Wittrock, eds, *Frontiers of sociology*, Leiden: Brill, 2009.

Henningsen, Manfred, *Der Mythos Amerika*, Frankfurt/M: Eichborn, 2009.

Hirschman, Albert, *The passions and the interests*, Princeton: Princeton Universiy Press, 1977

Holston, James, *Insurgent citizenship: disjunctions of democracy and modernity in Brazil*, Princeton: Princeton UP 2008.

Honneth, Axel, 'Das Gewebe der Gerechtigkeit. Über die Grenzen des zeitgenössischen Prozeduralismus', *Westend. Neue Zeitschrift für Sozialforschung*, vol. 6, 2010, no. 2, 3–22.

Honneth, Axel, *Verdinglichung. Eine anerkennungstheoretische Studie*, Frankfurt/M: Suhrkamp, 2005.

Honneth, Axel, 'Gerechtigkeit und kommunikative Freiheit. Überlegungen im Anschluß an Hegel', in: Barbara Merker, Georg Mohr and Michael Quante, eds, *Subjektivität und Anerkennung. Festschrift für Ludwig Siep*, Paderborn: Mentis, 2004.

Honneth, Axel, *Kampf um Anerkennung*, Frankfurt/M: Suhrkamp, 1992.

Joerges, Christian, Bo Stråth and Peter Wagner, eds, *The economy as a polity. The political constitution of contemporary capitalism*, London: UCL Press, 2005.

Jubber, Ken, 'Sociology in South Africa: a brief historical review of research and publishing', *Sociology*, 2007, Vol. 22, No. 5, 527–546.

Karagiannis, Nathalie, 'Multiple solidarities', in Karagiannis, Nathalie, and Peter Wagner, eds, *Varieties of world-making. Beyond globalization*, Liverpool: Liverpool UP, 2007.

Karagiannis, Nathalie, *Avoiding responsibility. The politics and discourse of EU development policy*, London: Pluto, 2004.

Karagiannis, Nathalie, and Peter Wagner, 'The liberty of the moderns compared to the liberty of the ancients', in Johann P. Arnason, Kurt Raaflaub and Peter Wagner, eds, *The Greek polis and the invention of democracy: a politico-cultural transformation and its interpretations*, Oxford: Blackwell, forthcoming, 2011

Karagiannis, Nathalie, and Peter Wagner, 'Varieties of agonism: conflict, the common good and the need for synagonism', *Journal of Social Philosophy*, vol. 39, no. 3, fall 2008.

Karagiannis, Nathalie, and Peter Wagner, eds, *Varieties of world-making. Beyond globalization*, Liverpool: Liverpool UP, 2007.

Kaya, Ibrahim, *Social theory and later modernities. The Turkish experience*, Liverpool: Liverpool University Press, 2004

Koselleck, Reinhart, *Kritik und Krise*, Freiburg: Alber, 1959

Koselleck, Reinhart, *Vergangene Zukunft*, Frankfurt/M.: Suhrkamp, 1979.

Lake, Marilyn, *Equality and exclusion: the racial constitution of colonial liberalism*, Thesis Eleven 2008, no. 95: 20–32.

Larrain, Jorge, 'Latin American varieties of modernity', in Nathalie Karagiannis and Peter Wagner, eds, *Varieties of world-making. Beyond globalization*, Liverpool: Liverpool UP, 2007.

Larrain, Jorge, *Identity and modernity in Latin America*, Cambridge: Polity, 2000.

Lefort, Claude, *La complication*, Paris: Fayard, 1999

Lefort, Claude, 'La question de la démocratie', in *Essais sur le politique. XIXe-XXe siècles*, Paris. Seuil, 1986, 17–30.

Lyotard, Jean-François, *La Condition postmoderne*. Paris: Minuit, 1979 (trans. G Bennington and B Massumi, *The Postmodern Condition* Manchester: Manchester University Press, 1994).

Mann, Michael, *The sources of social power*, Cambridge: Cambridge UP, vol. 1, 1986; vol. 2, 1993.

Morse, Richard M. The heritage of Latin America, in Louis Hartz, *The founding of new societies*, San Diego: Harcourt, Brace, Jovanovich, 1964, pp. 123–77.

Myrdal, Gunnar, *An American dilemma: The negro problem and modern democracy*, New York: Harper, 1944.

Noiriel, Gérard, *La tyrannie du national*, Paris: Calmann-Lévy, 1991.

Outhwaite, William, *The future of society*, Oxford: Blackwell, 2005.

Parsons, Talcott, 'Evolutionary universals in society', *American sociological review* 29, June, 1964.

Pocock, J.G.A., *The Machiavellian moment*, Princeton: Princeton UP, 1975.

Polanyi, Karl, *The Great Transformation*, Boston: Beacon, 1985 [1944].

Pomeranz, Kenneth, *The great divergence. China, Europe, and the making of the modern world economy*, Princeton: Princeton University Press, 2000.

Raaflaub, Kurt A., 'Perfecting the "Political Creature" (*zôion politikon*): 'Equality and "the Political" in the Evolution of Greek Democracy', in Johann P. Arnason, Kurt Raaflaub and Peter Wagner, eds, *The Greek polis and the invention of democracy: a politico-cultural transformation and its interpretations*, Oxford: Blackwell, forthcoming, 2011.

Rawls, John, *A theory of justice*, Cambrdige, MA: Bleknap Press of Harvard University press, 1971.

Rorty, Richard, *Contingency, irony, solidarity*, Cambridge: Cambridge University Press, 1989.

Salais, Robert, and Michael Storper, *Les mondes du production*, Paris: Editions de l'EHESS, 1993.

Santos, Boaventura de Sousa (ed.), *Reinventing social emancipation*, London: Verso, 2006-07 (three vols.).

Schiavone, Aldo, *La storia spezzata*, Rome/Bari: Laterza, 1996.

Schmidt, Volker H., 'Modernity and diversity', *Social Science Information*, vol. 49, no. 4, 2010, forthcoming.

Schwartzman, Simon, 'Changing roles of new knowledge: research institutions and societal transformations in Brazil', in *Social sciences and modern states*, ed. by Peter Wagner et al., Cambridge Cambridge UP, 1991.

Sewell, William H. jr., *Logics of history: social theory and social transformations*, Chicago:

The University of Chicago Press, 2005

Sewell, William H. jr., *Work and revolution in France*, Cambridge: Cambridge University Press, 1980.

Skinner, Quentin, 'Meaning and understanding in the history of ideas' (1969), now in: James Tully, ed., *Meaning and context. Quentin Skinner and his critics*, Cambridge: Cambridge UP, 1988, 29-67.

Smelser, Neil, *Problematics of sociology*. Berkeley: University of California Press, 1997.

Taylor, Charles, *Modern social imaginaries*, Durham, NC: Duke UP, 2005.

Taylor, Charles, *Sources of the self*, Cambridge, Mass.: Belknap Press of Harvard University Press, 1989.

Thompson, Leonard, *A history of South Africa*, Johannesburg/Cape Town, 2000.

Thompson, Leonard M., The South African dilemma, in Louis Hartz, *The founding of new societies*, San Diego: Harcourt, Brace, Jovanovich, 1964, pp. 178–218.

Touraine, Alain, *Critique de la modernité*. Paris: Fayard, 1992.

Wagner, Peter, The future of sociology: understanding the transformations of the social, in *The history and development of sociology*, ed. by Charles Crothers, Paris: UNESCO and EOLSS, forthcoming 2010.

Wagner, Peter, *Modernity as experience and interpretation. A new sociology of modernity*, Cambridge: Polity, 2008.

Wagner, Peter, 'Palomar's questions. The axial age hypothesis, European modernity and historical contingency' in Johann Arnason, Shmuel Eisenstadt and Björn Wittrock, eds., *Axial civilizations and world history*, Leiden: Brill Publishers, 2005, 87–106.

Wagner, Peter, *Theorizing modernity*, London: Sage, 2001

Wagner, Peter, *A sociology of modernity. Liberty and discipline*, London: Routledge, 1994.

Walzer, Michael, *Che cosa significa essere americani*, Padova: Marsilio, 2nd ed., 2001.

Yack, Bernard, *The fetishism of modernities*. Notre Dame: The University of Notre Dame Press, 1997.

Ypi, Lea L., 'Statist cosmopolitanism', *The Journal of Political Philosophy*, vol. 16, no. 1, 2008, 48–71.